EXCELLENCE IN PARTS WORK

Multiple Approaches and Proven Techniques for Helping Clients in Counseling, Coaching, and Hypnotherapy

Dr. Richard K. Nongard

www.ExpertHypnosis.com

Excellence in Parts Work: Multiple Approaches and Proven Techniques for Helping Clients in Counseling, Coaching, and Hypnotherapy

ISBN: 978-1-7344678-8-8

Dr. Richard K. Nongard

Cover design by Pankaj Singh Renu

First Printing: July 2022

This book is not intended as a substitute for therapeutic advice of a Licensed Professional. The reader should consult a mental health professional in matters relating to his/her individual mental health needs.

About Dr. Richard K. Nongard

Dr. Richard K. Nongard is a Licensed Marriage and Family Therapist and is a popular conference and keynote speaker known for his relaxed and engaging style. His focus is on real-world solutions based on the science of leadership, NLP, life coaching, and counseling psychology. His presentations focus on engagement, and actionable strategies for personal transformation.

He works as a professional hypnotist and life coach, helping people make rapid change in their health, wealth, and habits. He holds a Doctorate in Transformational Leadership (Cultural Transformation) from Bakke Graduate University. He also has an earned M.B.A. in Business Marketing and a M.A. in Counseling. He is currently completing a second doctorate, his Doctor of Psychology degree at California Southern University.

Richard is the author of numerous books, publications, and training videos. His book on leadership, *Viral Leadership: How to Seize the Power of Now to Create Lasting Transformation in Business*, has already become a popular resource for leadership development. He has written many other books as well, including psychology textbooks that have been adapted as textbooks at the university level, and his 5-star reviews are a testament to the value Richard provides in both written and spoken media.

Dr. Richard K. Nongard is a coach, consultant, and lecturer, offering services to individuals, communities, and healthcare organizations. You can bring him to your organization to train your executives or front-line employees in Leadership, Appreciative Inquiry and/or Emotional Intelligence.

To bring Dr. Richard K. Nongard to your organization or conference as a keynote speaker, contact him at ExpertHypnosis.com or (702) 418-3332.

You may download additional free resources for this book at:

ExpertHypnosis.com/optparts

To earn your certification as an ICBCH Certified Professional Hypnotist, Professional NLP Practitioner, or as a Professional Life Coach, visit:

ExpertHypnosis.com

Some of the many other books by

Dr. Richard K. Nongard

Excellence in NLP and Life Coaching

Speak Ericksonian: Mastering the Hypnotic Methods of Milton Erickson

Dr. Richard Nongard's Big Book of Hypnosis Scripts

The Self-Hypnosis Solution: Step-by-Step Methods and Scripts to Create Profound Change and Lifelong Results

The Seven Most Effective Methods of Self-Hypnosis: How to Create Rapid Change in your Health, Wealth, and Habits

Reframing Hypnotherapy: Evidence-Based Techniques for Your Next Hypnosis Session

Magic Words in Hypnosis: The Sourcebook Of Hypnosis Patter and Scripts And How To Overcome Hypnotic Difficulties

Advanced Parallel Programming and the Law of Attraction: How to Share the Law of Attraction and Bring Abundance to the People You Love

Viral Leadership: Seize the Power of Now to Create Lasting Transformation in Business

**Many additional books by Dr. Nongard
are available from any book retailer.**

Table of Contents

INTRODUCTION

This book is very practical and educational for those working in a variety of different traditions. You may have a background in psychotherapy or counseling. Or perhaps you are a life coach or come from a neuro-linguistic programming (NLP) perspective which often uses parts work just like counseling does. In the world of hypnosis, we know that parts work has been a central strategy or a central theme in most of our work.

Hypnotists, NLP practitioners, counselors, and psychotherapists each do parts work in their own way. My observation is that they do it in three different ways and that the different ways rarely cross over. They don't necessarily recognize when each other is using parts work. The NLP practitioner looks at the others and says, "What kind of parts work is that? That is not what parts work is." Let me assure you that there are many sections to parts work. In this book, I will address all the different sections.

I will share specific strategies for parts work, ego state theory, and internal family systems (IFS). I have a counseling, Ericksonian, and indirect hypnosis background. If you have a counseling or psychotherapy background, you will recognize the idea of parts work, ego state theory, and IFS as being a component of some of the work you have already done. You will be able to increase your skills, so when you have a client in your office, you can use the concepts from this book to directly impact them.

In addition to the idea of parts work being a core of psychotherapy, it has also long been a core technique in professional hypnosis, neuro-linguistic programming, and life coaching. As a professional hypnotist, when I work with individuals, the value of doing parts work in my sessions is amazing. Parts work, and the techniques and the ideas that I will share with you are flexible and adaptable.

Many people have transitioned their business models over the past couple of years. They have moved from doing in-person office sessions to working with clients online. The good news is that parts work is adaptable for in-person and online client sessions or any other form of telecommunication. These strategies are flexible and adaptable. You will find that no matter what your background, there is a strategy and a technique that will be useful to you and the clients you work with.

The best part, though, is that you are going to personally benefit from the material in this book. I want you to learn and understand the ideas of parts therapy and know the techniques. I also want you to practice this in self-hypnosis or in your quiet time. I want you to apply the techniques that I will be sharing with you to your own life first. This means that you can work honestly with your clients and passionately share with them. That is a great position to be in when working with clients.

CHAPTER ONE:

The Id, The Ego, and the Super-Ego

The starting point for parts therapy, ego state therapy, and internal family systems began in 1923 with Sigmund Freud. Our first conceptualization of the human psyche was Sigmund Freud's idea. Because of those ideas, I will use the words "parts work," "ego state therapy," and "internal family systems," and I use them fairly interchangeably. However, regardless of your perspective, you will find that the ideas really overlap because they all originated with Sigmund Freud and his ideas on the human psyche.

The ideas that Freud articulated a hundred years ago are ideas that are pervasive and continue in the worlds of therapy, NLP, and professional hypnosis. Freud identified the first three parts: the id, the ego, and the superego. Below I discuss each of these aspects or parts of the human psyche.

The Id: Freud also gave us the core concept of hypnosis, expressing the mind as conscious, preconscious, superconscious, or unconscious. He gave us the idea that we have both a conscious mind and an unconscious mind. He also gave us the idea of parts; the three parts of the human mind and the human psyche.

The id is the primitive—the "old mind." This is the selfish part of the mind. It is the part that is protective. This is the part where reproduction, sex, aggression, and hunger reside. The id is the demanding part of our human psyche or personality. It is impulsive and animalistic.

Whenever Fred Flintstone from the television cartoon *The Flintstones* had a decision to make, on one side of his shoulder was a little devil friend who would pop up and tell him what to do. That is the id—the devil sitting on your shoulder. It is filled with drive, is unrelenting, and wants what it wants. A baby behaves in this manner. The id is the first part of the human psyche to develop. Its goal is to get our needs met at any cost.

Freud's ideas, can be conceptualized as an iceberg.

The id is the primitive part of the mind, operating out of what Freud called an unconscious level. This is the primitive, the selfish, the protective, the aggressive part of the mind.

The Ego: The ego is you, that part of you that is in the middle of the devil on your shoulder and the angel on your other shoulder. This part of us mediates between conflict—the internal conflict between the id and the superego. This is the part of us that in parts theory is sometimes referred to as the "executive"—the one making decisions. This is the part that strives to reduce impulsiveness or internal conflict. This is the part of us that is rational, logical, and that thinks things through. The id acts quickly, and the ego sometimes works slowly. It functions as the mediator or the control between the conflict of the superego and the id.

The Superego: The superego is the part of the mind that is idealistic. It's a part of who we are—our personality with morals or values. This part of us says, "It is wrong to steal. It is wrong to kill other people." It is also the part of us that says, "I should watch somebody in traffic in front of me." This is the ethical part of us—the role of the judge.

The superego comes in when the id says, "I want something now" and says, "This is either right or wrong. This is good or bad." It is the part of our personality that is the parent role. You have likely heard the idea of self-parenting and learning to self-parent. It is really about developing the superego. This is where our values lie—our core values. Whenever Fred Flintstone had a debate, there was a devil on one shoulder—his id. The angel friend on his other shoulder, his superego, was telling him the right thing to do so that he did not upset Wilma too much.

The superego is the moral-ethical part of the iceberg. You will notice in the iceberg graphic that we have our conscious minds, and we have what Freud called the preconscious mind. This is what is on our minds right now. The conscious mind is what is happening in this moment— the decisions, the actions, and the experiences that we are having right now. We can easily bring the preconscious mind to any situation. You can conceptualize the preconscious mind as being on the tip of your tongue and the tip of your mind. Part of the superego, as well as the ego, is in this preconscious part. It resides in the unconscious mind, but it is at the top and is always ready to be accessed. That is an important thing that we are going to come back to later on, but this is who the superego is.

With this idea of the mind being in the brain, I want to stress that the idea of the conscious mind, the unconscious mind, or the subconscious mind are only metaphors anyway. Mind resides in more than just our brain. Mind is actually and literally in every cell of our body. When someone draws a representation of a mind, they always draw the brain. The entire central nervous system going all the way down to the spine could be a representation of the mind and probably in each and every cell of our body as well.

Let's see how this works. The id says, "I'm hungry."

The ego says, "I'm going to leave this meeting early, and I'm going to go eat a sandwich."

The superego says, "Oh, wait a minute. If you do that, people will think you are rude or uninterested. You probably should wait until we are done."

That is just one example of the id, the ego, and the superego working together.

Let's take a look at another idea here and put it in the context of hypnosis. The id says, "I have to stop this negative feeling right now, so I am going to use (drugs, alcohol, tobacco, impulsive sex, impulsive shopping, emergency anxiety coping strategies) to get what I need right here in this minute."

The ego comes along and says, "Well, Richard, you probably shouldn't be so impulsive and drink that twelve-pack of beer."

The superego comes along and says, "This is not something that is consistent with your values or something that you want to do."

So we have the id saying, "I have got to find a solution right now." The superego says, "You need to repress or subjugate those desires." And the ego is trying to find the balance.

Put this in context with the clients you work with in hypnosis or coaching. These clients are looking for that balance.

We need our needs met. We need our desires to be fulfilled, but we need to do it in the context of the bigger picture. It is the ego that helps us to moderate. When we are working with clients, we are almost always equipping the ego with a set of skills and strategies to navigate the different conflicts deep within.

The interesting thing about Freud's iceberg analogy here is that the unconscious mind is the biggest part of the iceberg. Most of what is going on is occurring without conscious awareness—maybe in the preconscious part of the mind—that could come to our awareness at any point. But no matter what is going on in our world, this is always who I am. On the diagram, you will notice a red line illustrating that the id, ego, and superego are working simultaneously across Freud's division of the conscious mind, preconscious mind, and unconscious mind. This was Freud's eminent theory or idea. Probably his greatest contribution was to organize the field of psychology.

Sigmund Freud spent a lot of time writing about many cases, theories, and ideas. In his later life, he discarded most of his theories and ideas, retaining only the id, the ego, and the superego, after his lifetime of study as one of those things he conceptualized as valid and useful. It is his greatest contribution to our understanding of psychotherapy, counseling, hypnosis, and NLP.

Think about the work that you do. It is about helping people to create balance with those inner conflicts. We cannot actually change the past. We cannot impact the future because it hasn't happened yet. Almost always, we cannot change other people's experiences or interactions. We only have the ability to change ourselves. "God grant me the courage to change the things I can." We are trying to help them find that balance, accept the things they can, and live fully in the present.

Freud's idea of the id, the ego, and the superego combine to create a psychodynamic approach to the human psyche. Even though we might use cognitive behavioral therapy, mindfulness-based stress reduction, solution-focused family therapy, direct hypnosis, NLP ecology checks, or all these other things we have learned, our work's foundation is still a hundred years post-Freud. Certainly, the aspects of internal family systems theory, the ideas of parts work, and ego state therapy are all psychodynamic in orientation. This means we can work with our clients to help them reconcile the battle between these three parts— the id, the ego, and the superego.

I hope you can see that these ideas have been pervasive no matter what language we use or what tradition we come from. They will be useful for us as we now explore the different elements or aspects of each of the modern-day approaches in parts work that we might use.

CHAPTER TWO:

Different Understandings of Parts Work and Ego-States

I n this chapter, I will provide you with several different theories or systems of understanding parts work and ego states from which we will create interventions.

When I have a client in my office, I am not a one-size-fits-all person. I want to match the ideas or the strategies that will uniquely help that person based on a broad set of knowledge. That is why when we engage in something as significant as studying parts work or parts therapy, we want to understand the history, various viewpoints, advantage points, and how they are different. We can then, of course, create interventions for our unique clients. They will be based on those unique aspects of the different types of knowledge we have. For example, Sigmund Freud was a psychoanalyst who looked at the content of a person's experience and tried to help a person understand and create understanding from within that content.

In transactional analysis, the experience here is a little bit different. You will see some overlaps between the id, the ego, and the superego and what Eric Berne wrote about when he described the processes of transactional analysis. In transactional analysis, we're not looking at the content of the experience. Instead, we're trying to alter the ego states of the communicator so that we can change emotions. After all, communication coming from an ego state is not quite as resourceful. They're having difficulties in their various relationships, social experiences, or emotions.

Transactional analysis is a communication strategy. It almost fits or overlaps with some of what we know about neuro-linguistic programming. Of course, it is something that hypnotists have been using for years to enhance the experience of creating more effective hypnosis sessions. Let's look at some of the basic elements of transactional analysis and how it relates to parts therapy.

The Ego State

An ego state is something that is consistent. That is first and foremost. This is something that emerges or replicates itself across a variety of different situations. An ego state, according to Berne, is described as the consistent pattern of feeling and experience that directly relates to a corresponding behavior. Regardless of whether the behavior is aggression or addiction, or the behavior is acceptable, there is a consistent feeling and experience directly related to it across the broad spectrum of different situations.

In transactional analysis, they identify ego states dealing with consistent patterns of feelings and experiences that people have related to their behavior. These contain the behaviors that people have, the thoughts that people have, their feelings or emotions, values and beliefs, and cultural experience or the rules of life they have.

These states dictate the communication we will have with other people, and I would like to point out the communication—the internal dialogue—that we have with ourselves. Let me give you an example here because, in transactional analysis, we are talking about three ego states; the parent ego state, the adult ego state, and the child ego state. The parent might be the person who communicates by yelling. The child might be the person who communicates by sulking. The adult is the person who might choose acceptance to let go of something so that they can be fully in the present. Below, I explore these ego states and some of the characteristics of each one.

The Parent

The parent ego state develops due to our interactions with our parents, caregivers, and teachers—the authorities and the adults in the world around us when we are small children. The parent ego state that we develop is modeled from learning other people's communication styles in a parent and used broadly in a parent role. It is a replay of the previous learnings that we have and what we think a parent role or authority role would be doing in different situations and how they would communicate. The aspects of this could be nurturing or critical.

You probably heard it said that we only know what we know. If you come from a family of trauma, a family with adverse childhood experiences, or a family with traumas, the chances are good that the model you have for a parent did not necessarily equip you with effective communication strategies for effective parenting. I don't mean just in the context of your children. I mean, in the context of when you are parenting employees, parenting other people you are leading. In a wide variety of different situations, you might step into a parent role even in interacting with other adults.

This parent ego state is a collection of learned communications that we have that impact how we interact and relate to others in the world around us. You will notice that transactional analysis, in addition to being a model of communication, is also a model of personality development. They are consistent feelings and experiences that draw from a wide range of behaviors, thoughts, feelings, values, life rules, and cultural experiences.

The Adult

This ego state steps into a logical, thoughtful, and adaptive frame of reference. The adult differs from the parent, and that parent ego state is a replay of what we know that the parent role does. It is implied to us by what we observed. But the adult ego state is the ego state that is mindful. It is the one that is in the present. It is the one who can let go of past learnings and be adaptive to the present situation. This is what breaks the cycle of families repeating themselves. It is a person developing a strong ego state of their adult. The goal of the adult ego state is the acceptance of reality. Some of you come from a therapy background and are probably familiar with William Glasser and his ideas and landmark book on psychotherapy called *Reality Therapy*.

Actually, the goal of the adult ego state is experiencing reality in the present. I come from a tradition or a school of thought that focuses on acceptance and commitment therapy. That is called contextual psychology. Contextual psychology, of course, wants to stay in the present moment. My favorite quote is from the Great Master Oogway, the turtle from the *Kung Fu Panda* movie. "Yesterday is history. Tomorrow is a mystery. But today is a gift. That is why it is called the present." It is the adult that understands the profound words of the Great Master Oogway.

The Child

The child ego state is free and adaptive. It can be flexible and experience new things, and it can be creative. Interestingly, the child ego state is a replay of our own experiences. Think about your own childhood experiences. Some of those experiences were wonderful. Some of those experiences may have been tragic. The reality is we only know what it is that we know.

The child ego state is our collection of life's scripts. The child ego state is the first to develop because, as children, we experience the world around us, moving into the development of the parent ego state as we observe those authorities around us whom we learn from. With the right set of tools, we develop the adult ego state and can maybe discard all the previously learned ideas and step into new experiences to take risks because it is seen as beneficial in the present moment.

In transactional analysis, we also have the four vantage points or viewpoints of how we relate to the world around us with these various ego states. The first psychology book I ever read was Thomas Harris's *I'm OK—You're OK*. It was written as a self-help book and was based on the ideas of transactional analysis.

Transactional analysis as a communication strategy was profoundly influential to me as a young person. Some of the core ideas of transactional analysis underlie some of my ideas.

Transactional analysis groups were very, very popular. John Denver wrote about his experience with transactional analysis in his autobiography *Take Me Home*. And the book *The Celestine Prophecy* by James Redfield touches on experiences of transactional analysis. You can see this has been an influential set of ideas for a long period of time.

There are four vantage points:

"I'm OK, you're OK"

This is considered the healthiest of all the vantage points. It's when I see other people as being equal to me. I'm interested in sharing respect with them, listening to them, giving to them, and receiving from them. The reason why is that my communication values other people, but I also see myself as valued. There is something magnificent about healthy relationships.

During my training as a marriage and family therapist, the idea of transactional analysis as a tool for couples' communication was certainly being taught at that time. The vantage point of a healthy marriage is, "I'm OK, you're OK." This is considered the most valuable or most desired vantage point. But for various reasons, in transactional analysis, we would probably say that because the corresponding behavior of a person's experiences is not consistent with these belief sets or viewpoints, we can find ourselves with one of the other vantage points.

"I'm okay, but you're not okay"

This is where communication discounts other people. It views other people as being less than. "I view myself as being superior." You can see, of course, right off the bat, what is wrong with this. Think about the people you have had to communicate with over the years—bosses, colleagues, coworkers, family, friends, stepparents, next-door neighbors, whoever it is that is in your world. If you ever had the viewpoint, "I'm okay, but you're not okay," this is not considered to be a healthy framework or state of mind.

"I'm not okay, but you are"

We see this vantage point in many people. This is where an inferiority complex or lack of confidence comes from. As a hypnotist, I see a lot of people who wish to improve their confidence. They might come to me and say, "I need confidence for stage fright." Or "I need the confidence to be able to do public speaking." Or "I need confidence in my relationships to stand up for myself." They are really saying that they believe, "I'm not okay, but you're okay." This is another unhealthy element of how people see themselves.

"I'm not okay and you're not okay"

This is Harris's last belief set. This is fatalistic and is a hopeless state. Think again about the people in the world around you who you have interacted with. Many people have concluded, "You know what? The world isn't okay, but I'm not okay either." They've given up and do not believe there is actually hope. And so, the goal of transactional analysis is to alter the communication that we have from our ego states to change our emotions so that we move to a healthy vantage point where we believe and interact with the world as if "I'm okay and you're okay" as well.

In transactional analysis and in this model of ego states, we have some presuppositions. If you have come to hypnosis from a background of NLP, you are probably familiar with the NLP presuppositions. In my book, *Excellence in NLP and Life Coaching*, I wrote about the presuppositions in the first part of the book. These are the operating assumptions that we have as NLP practitioners and, in many cases, as hypnotists, that we simply accept as fact.

Sometimes in the NLP presuppositions, we might have a hard time accepting their validity, yet we operate as if they are true. It is the same thing in transactional analysis. There are some fundamental presuppositions so when we work with clients to help them alter their ego states with more effective communication so that they can change their emotional experience and move from anger or hostility into acceptance and joy, we are going to work with them with a framework that has certain presuppositions.

Transactional Analysis Presupposition No. 1: People are okay.

This is a really important presupposition because it is important to recognize that while people may be different from us, or may have experiences that are different from us, or might even have problems that are not problems, a client-centered approach where we see people as simply being okay is important because your clients are going to pick up from you a judgment. Your clients are going to pick up from you a discomfort. Your clients are going to pick up from you feelings that, on a subconscious level, you communicate to them maybe from a parent role or maybe from a child role ego state that do not really see them as being okay.

I had an experience years ago. I was doing a lot of training with the probation department systems in the 1990s. I had a group at Corpus

Christi made up of social workers, marriage and family therapists, psychotherapists, and licensed professional counselors. There were substance abuse counselors and probation officers in the audience. At that particular time, I worked as a substance abuse counselor in a substance abuse treatment program. My clients were substance abuse patients in a sex offender treatment program in state custody. That was the work that I was doing at the time. I was doing a workshop with this group, not about substance abuse and not about sex offenders. But of course, I mentioned my work as a substance abuse counselor working in the sex offender treatment program. One of the ladies in the group said, "Oh my gosh, how can you work with those people?"

I thought about it for a minute and responded that I could work with those people because even though they've done awful things, and even though they should be held responsible for their behavior, at my core, I really do try to live by the grace of God. I see that spark of the divine in other people. I look for that rather than what is wrong with them. I have met many people who have a lot of things wrong with them. They are not okay in many different ways in life, but I have never met anybody yet who did not have something okay with them. And so, transactional analysis starts with the presupposition that people are okay.

Transactional Analysis Presupposition No. 2: Positive Reinforcement

This presupposition is the most effective way to help somebody make a change. In hypnosis, we want to give positive suggestions rather than negative suggestions. This is why I do not use any or every little aversion therapy in my work. Positive reinforcement tends to help people make change more effectively.

Transactional Analysis Presupposition No 3: People Have a Capacity for Love

In his book *Reality Therapy*, William Glasser wrote that our greatest or deepest need is to love other people and be able to receive love in return.

I told a story recently about one of my experiences in Kyiv, Ukraine. When I was in Kyiv, I was with my friend Pavel, and we were walking down Khreschatyk Street. It was 2004, and we were walking to the train station past the break-dancers with street performers playing Frank Sinatra's *My Way*. Past McDonald's, past the beautiful sights in what I think is one of the most beautiful cities in Europe. I was asked a question, "Are Ukrainians like Americans?"

I thought about it for a while before I answered. I thought about my experiences earlier that week with old uncle Victor, who couldn't understand I wasn't going to have a shot of vodka with him to help celebrate Babushka's birthday. We later came to an agreement that I would drink Bonaqua water, and he would have vodka, and we would celebrate together. I had traveled there many times and spent some time in a city called Uman, one of the most beautiful places I have ever been to. I thought about the people I had met—my friend Sarah Jane, my friend Igor, and some of the other people I was with. I answered the question, "Yes, Ukrainians are just like Americans. They all want the same two things. They want freedom, and they want love. And so, yes, Ukrainians are just like Americans."

People have the capacity for love. Transactional analysis recognizes this. This is one of the foundations for being able to work with very difficult clients. How do you work with difficult clients recognizing that all people are not loving? People have the capacity to meet their deepest needs, love, and freedom. Transactional analysis recognizes the power of the mind.

Transactional Analysis Presupposition No. 4: People Think, and our Thoughts Lead to Actions

Transactional analysis says that there is a facet of each one of these ego states that has value. One is not better than another. They can be accessed in different situations to communicate in different ways. But we need that child within. We need that parent role to set boundaries and live a healthy life. We need the adult role to be logical and to be based on the present. And so, each one of these ego states, each one of these facets has value for us, and one is not better than the other. Transactional analysis tells us that people decide their story. Because of that, people have the ability to change their stories.

Transactional Analysis Presupposition No. 5: All Emotional Difficulties can be Resolved

There is hope for everybody using the tools that transactional analysis gives us to help us communicate more effectively so that we can alter our ego states and change our emotions by operating from a parent that is nurturing, healthy, giving, compassionate, and caring; from an adult ego state that is present-minded and patient; and from a child perspective that is free, explores, and allows us to continue to be creative even into our old age.

In my next chapter, I will be sharing with you some of the ideas from the internal family systems theory.

CHAPTER THREE:

Ideas from Internal Family Systems

In this chapter, I will share with you some of the components for conceptualizing parts therapy that the internal family system (IFS) theory shares that are particularly useful to the hypnotist. This is a great way to conceptualize the different parts and subparts of our personalities. Freud's main idea, of course, was that we can observe these personality characteristics—the id, the ego, and the superego—so we can understand them.

Richard Schwartz developed the internal family systems theory in the 1980s. In the 1990s, he wrote great books on the subject. He conceptualizes the importance of parts a little bit differently. Rather than coming to an understanding of these things, what Schwartz asks us to do is actually have the parts befriend, speak to, and communicate with the other parts. He says that this is how healing takes place and that one of the problems with individuals is that their parts are not communicating.

You can conceptualize this as family therapy. As a licensed family therapist, this really resonates with me. If I'm doing a family therapy session and I have a mother, father, two children, and grandma in the room with me, there may be disagreement or miscommunication between some family members. For example, grandma and the daughter might be triangulating with the mother and older brother or other dynamics like that.

What Schwartz says is that this is literally what our personalities are doing. Parts of our personalities are not communicating and functioning well with the other parts of our families. In family therapy, to resolve an issue between the couple, you might actually bring the other family members in and work with just them. Then there might be a time to integrate that family at a higher level of functioning by bringing them back in after resolving the issue with those individuals. In parts therapy, what we are doing is an IFS approach to therapy. We are teaching our personality parts to become aware and communicate with and speak to one another. This promotes openness and promotes integration, health, healing, and wellness.

Let's take a look at the different parts that Schwartz gives us. The first one is, of course, the self. According to IFS, we are born with a self, and this self has eight characteristics, all denoted with the letter C:

1. Calmness
2. Curiosity
3. Creativity
4. Confidence
5. Connectedness
6. Clarity
7. Courage
8. Compassion

The idea here is that we are all born with this self—this part or personality—that ideally encompasses these healthy mechanisms of healthy functioning. What happens to all of us, and I mean all of us and not just the clients we work with, is that we experience traumas. Some people experience severe trauma, some unexpected traumas, and others trauma as they simply go through the different developmental stages because life itself is traumatic.

I think one of the things we should be doing in our work is normalizing the experience of trauma. That does not mean we endorse it or we are glad that difficult or bad things happen to people, but we need to recognize that trauma is actually the normal state of the human experience. Life is traumatic. This is one of the reasons why I have never really been a fan of regression to cause, which looks for the cause of a problem or behavior.

The reality is that life is the cause of these problems and behaviors. Most of my clients have multiple traumas. But as children, when we start to experience these traumas, to retain a sense of homeostasis or equilibrium, we exile those parts of our personality. The IFS approach labels these exiles, and they include body sensations.

You may have read the book *The Body Keeps the Score* by Bessel van der Kolk. We literally store trauma in our bodies—which resonates with me—because the mind is not just the brain. Mind is in every cell of our body. And so, it is no surprise since the mind is in every cell of our body that our thoughts are felt somatically. Emotions can be exiled—intense, unwanted, difficult, and even pleasurable emotions. Our urges are a component of the exiles. The drives that we have and the beliefs that we have all become a part of an exile personality. Within the exile, there are numerous subpersonalities that encompass these different elements of the personality.

In IFS, we now only have the self that we are born with that is impacted by the experience of trauma creating these exiles. The reason why these exiles are there is that we want to put some space between our trauma and our experiences in order to be able to function. Imagine even thinking about the traumas you have experienced in your life, if some time had not gone by, some emotional healing had not been done, and we had become fused to those traumas, we wouldn't be able to function. That is literally what is happening to many of our clients. They become fused to their traumas. The exiles are not doing a bad thing. They are only doing what they know how to do, and they are doing the best they can with their tools.

The IFS gives us two other ego states or personality parts that we have to become familiar with. The first of these is the manager. This is the part of us that, in response to these exiles, is trying to suppress the unhealthy or dysfunctional aspects of the exile personality. The manager is the part of our personality trying to create survival in what really is truly a chaotic world. There are different aspects of how we might manage or how we might suppress the exiles—maybe through our religious experiences and beliefs, through anxiety, fear, panic, and phobias that we develop.

None of these things are, in and of themselves, healthy or unhealthy. Religion can be a healthy way for people to understand the unexplainable. We all know that religion can also become an unhealthy way for some individuals to interact with the world around them in a way that isn't constructive. It's the same with exercise. Exercise is healthy, but we also know the person who exercises at the expense of other essential aspects of their life. It has almost become an addiction for them and something that has become unhealthy for them.

Depending on how they are manifested, any of these aspects of the manager's role can be healthy or unhealthy. Some people have a drive for success. They want to overcome a wounded self carrying an exile of defeat, hopelessness, or worthlessness and are trying to compensate for it with riches, wealth, and success.

It can be a way to manage the inner critic or the critic of the external world as well. We have all met the person who has nothing nice to say about others. The same thing is true with intellect or the pursuit of knowledge—the body experiences what people create.

The manager is trying to manage the more impulsive part of the personality, which is the exile. I know many readers are familiar with NLP. In NLP we have the first perceptual position, which is me in the middle of an experience. And the second perceptual position is me outside of me, observing me in that experience. We put some space between them. You can see how, even though these therapies and theories might have different names, they relate to various parts or elements of one another. We can use the ideas of IFS in hypnosis, in coaching, and in our work in NLP. We can also use it in our work in traditional therapy or counseling.

In addition to the manager, we also have the firefighter. The firefighter role comes in when the manager is unable to work with the exiles in a way that creates equilibrium or the self functioning at a healthy level. The firefighter's role is to distract us from pain or trauma. It is a reactive personality trait or personality part. It is reacting to the manager's inability to work with the exiles to create a sense of calm with the self. How does the firefighter do this? The firefighter might do this with both healthy and unhealthy actions and behaviors, experiences, and emotions—alcohol use, drug use, addiction, shopping addiction, rage, self-harm, impulsive behavior, and dissociating.

Dissociating seems to be something that is characterized as bad in the world of psychology. There are a number of different things that make up a person's experience with dissociation. It can be a numbing of the senses. It can be a lack of awareness of others as well as avoidance. Dissociation can also be a way of bringing ourselves out of experiences and situations—a way of putting some space between us and our traumas. So there are healthy and unhealthy aspects to each one of these.

One of the things that we need to recognize is that in IFS, the premise is that all these parts serve to protect us and help us to be our very best. But sometimes, these parts do not communicate with one another, are unknown to one another, or sometimes these parts have different motivations than other parts. By creating a dialogue with these parts, they can function in a way that helps to protect us.

What are some of the other presuppositions of the internal family systems theory? One of them is important for us to recognize because it ties into Milton Erickson's viewpoint.

Erickson had the viewpoint that the subconscious mind has all the resources needed to solve any problem, which is why when Erickson did hypnosis, he used some really creative interventions and suggestions. They weren't coming from him—they were coming from inside his clients. IFS shares the same philosophy: the true self with all eight Cs—calmness, curiosity, creativity, confidence, connectedness, clarity, courage, and compassion. It does exist. If we cannot see it, cannot manifest it, or cannot experience it, the reason is that traumas cloud it.

Internal Family Systems Theory Presupposition No. 1:

Understanding and befriending the different parts, creating dialogue and communication, leads to trauma resolution. This is in line with the ideas of acceptance commitment therapy. The idea is acceptance. Acceptance does not mean I liked or endorsed the bad things or the traumas. It does not even mean I'm glad it happened to me. Rather it simply means that I acknowledged their presence, their existence. IFS shares this similar vantage point that we understand and befriend the parts, that we honor the components of the part, which is trying to accomplish the eight Cs. And that when we do this, it leads to the resolution of trauma.

Internal Family Systems Theory Presupposition No. 2:

Confusion and frustration come from keeping these parts from communicating with one another, knowing one another, and speaking with one another.

This confusion and frustration create continued chaos which in turn contributes to more and more traumas. Of course, as I mentioned before, in internal family systems theory, the parts speak to each other.

In our hypnosis sessions, where we begin to draw the techniques from these various theories, we will ask our client's parts to speak to their other parts. This can be a powerful way to increase the experience and effectiveness of a hypnosis session and equip our clients to take powerful action on the posthypnotic suggestions because the posthypnotic suggestions do not come from me. They come from one part of the client to another. The manager is helping the firefighter; the firefighter is helping the manager. The manager and firefighter work with the exiles to create this self that has a sense of freedom, a sense of love, a sense of autonomy, and the ability to function at its highest level.

As we go into the next few chapters, I will share with you other approaches that utilize parts work and our understanding of the ego states of parts therapy. A lot of these terms are fairly interchangeable. Then we will begin creating some interventions based on each of them that we can use in our coaching, counseling, NLP, or hypnosis sessions.

CHAPTER FOUR:

Scripts and techniques

A client who does not know anything about the id, ego, the superego, or Sigmund Freud, shared with me their situation. "I do something that I know is not good for me. When I get upset or angry, I feel like I need to make myself feel better, so I go shopping and buy something. At that moment, after making a purchase, I feel good. But then I feel bad when I get home." The question posed to me was, "Why do I keep doing this?"

This graphic of the id, the ego, and the superego helps explain what is going on.

The id is the part of us that has that craving, the impulsivity. It says, "I don't feel good. I got to change this feeling." Some of my clients, for example, weight loss clients and addicts, say, "I've got to change this feeling."

The Big Book from Alcoholics Anonymous tells us that the reason people drink is not that it makes them feel better. Alcoholism might actually make people feel worse. According to *The Big Book*, the first 100 alcoholics who wrote in it drank because it made them feel different. It does not make them feel better. It might make them feel worse, but at least it makes them feel different. Addiction clients, compulsive shopping clients, weight loss clients, and many other clients have cravings and impulsivity in an attempt to change the feeling of not feeling good.

I used to be afraid to fly. There was no way I would get on a metal object painted like Shamu and be hurled through space at 600 miles an hour. I overcame my fear of flying a long time ago. I might even consider flying across the country just to eat lunch with someone. But in the past, I would panic with my fear of flying if I had to go anywhere. I just got to a point where I flat out wouldn't. That is the immature part. That is the id part.

In the shopping example, we have the part that is the id which is immature. It is impulsive, and it wants what it wants, and it wants it immediately.

The id goes out shopping and buys something, which makes the ego feel really happy. "Look, I bought this fancy ring." And then, the superego comes in and says, "Oh, wait a bit. That probably isn't good for your budget. Maybe you should return it. You shouldn't do that again," etc. We have a conflict with our different parts.

In doing a hypnosis session, the question is, "How can I use my knowledge of the id, the ego, and the superego to create an intervention or a script that can use this knowledge that I have?"

I am a big fan of both indirect and direct hypnosis. Indirect hypnosis is where we share in our hypnosis session in a way that causes the client to have an Aha! experience. They take the story, the parable, the metaphor, and the indirect suggestions we have given them, and a part of them understands at a subconscious level what is important to them from the story. Over the years, I have curated many different stories that I can share with my clients in indirect hypnosis.

One of my favorite sources for stories that can be used in hypnosis is Aesop's Fables. I do not share an Aesop fable with every client. But I have certainly found that by having a fable at the tip of my tongue at just about any point in any hypnosis session, I can have stories that teach truths to our clients. If you think, "Well, that sounds like a cool idea. I wish I knew where I could curate stories for the hypnotist that actually illustrate these points," Bob Martel wrote a book titled *The Magic of Aesop: How to Use the Wisdom of Aesop's Fables to Spark Transformational Change.*

One of the fables I love to draw from is *The Heron.*

Imagine you are my client, and we have completed our pre-talk, induction, and deepener; "5, 4, 3, 2, 1, 0. Now you are in this awesome place that we call hypnosis."

What I would probably do is begin with some indirect suggestions. I would say, "Congratulate yourself for coming here today. You've decided to make some changes that are important to you. But before we get to the point in our session where I am going to share with you some alternatives, I'm reminded of a story. That story is one that Aesop told us many years ago. It's the story of the heron.

A Heron was walking sedately along the bank of a stream, his eyes on the clear water and his long neck and pointed bill ready to snap up a likely morsel for his breakfast. The clear water swarmed with fish, but Master Heron was hard to please that morning.

'No small fry for me,' he said. 'Such scanty fare isn't fit for a heron.'

Now, a fine young perch swam near.

'No indeed,' said the Heron. 'I wouldn't even trouble to open my beak for anything like that!'

As the sun rose, the fish left the shallow water near the shore and swam below into the cool depths toward the middle. The Heron saw no more fish, and very glad was he at last to breakfast on a tiny Snail."

This is an illustration of the id, the ego, and the superego at work. The id says, "I'm hungry." The ego says, "You better get something good." And the superego says, "Do not be too hard to suit, or you might have to be content with the worst or nothing at all." This is the learning that comes from this story. You can see that indirect suggestion can be accomplished with a story or parable. It does not have to be something famous like one of Aesop's Fables. It can even be a story of your own experience.

If you were my client with an addiction to cocaine, I could add into a hypnosis session, "You know what's interesting as you have struggled with relapse and addiction? I am reminded of a client who, although not a cocaine addict like you, came to me and said, 'Why is it that I feel bad and buy something to feel good and then feel worse later on?' You have probably had this experience in your cocaine use where you used cocaine, saying to yourself, 'I'd like to feel better.' But it actually made you feel worse."

I can share a story about somebody else, whether that person was real or not, and have somebody develop insights into their own experiences. This is what the psychodynamic approach is all about. The psychodynamic approach is really about a person being able to generate insight into their own experiences. Freud's idea was that a client could see him every week for fifty weeks a year, leaving two weeks for vacation. At the end of ten years, the client will have developed so much insight that they would be a radically different person, but their personality would not change. That was Freud's idea.

Now we live in a managed-care world, so no one has ten years to work with a client, and because we live in 2022, no one has the attention span to wait ten years to solve their problems. The idea of the psychodynamic approach is to generate insight. This is consistent with Milton Erickson's idea that we have the tools to make a change within us. And so, sharing stories like this is one way to help a person understand their parts—the id, the ego, and the superego.

Unlike a story, this is a set of direct suggestions. In a session, I might deliver the induction, deepener, or indirect suggestion and then follow up with a direct suggestion. There is absolutely no reason why I need to keep Sigmund Freud secret.

Here's a script I wrote for a weight-loss client. This can help a person understand the id, the ego, and the superego. Again, imagine that the induction and deepener have already been delivered.

"As you continue to relax, in 3, 2, 1, 0, I am going to share with you some direct suggestions. That's what we in hypnosis call the things that I'm telling you to help you make changes. What's important about the suggestions that I'm going to be sharing with you is these aren't actually suggestions that I've created. They're not suggestions that come from me. They're actually suggestions that you've asked me to make for you by coming here today.

Really, any suggestions that I give you in our hypnosis session are actually suggestions that you've crafted, that you've created, and that have importance to you.

I bet you've heard of Sigmund Freud. Sigmund Freud gave us a theory of our personality. He identified three different parts—the id, the ego, and the superego. Each one of these parts plays a role in understanding our problems and solving them. It is nice to have a solution to a problem, especially one like weight loss.

After all, you've known that the excess weight you have is a problem. Now you can start solving it with this one simple trick. The id is that part of our personality that wants what it wants, and it wants it now, and sometimes it screams, 'Give me a custard-filled crepe or some salty snack.' But other times, the id simply says, 'Feed me.' The id is impulsive. It wants what it wants at that moment. You've probably said these things to yourself.

What happened? Chances are that minutes or hours later, when you saw a cake or some other automatic behavior triggered your awareness of food, this part of your personality said, 'Well, just one won't hurt,' or 'I'll put it off and start my weight loss tomorrow.' Freud would have told us that that was the superego trying to meet the urges of the moment. Interestingly, he said that this was the strongest part of our personality.

But another part of our personality is also at work. This is the superego and, unlike the devil (the id) on the shoulder, the superego is like an angel telling us, 'You better be good and go without,' or 'You'll only get celery tonight.' The problem here, of course, is this is the classic pattern for a diet, and that's probably failed you before, hasn't it? Of course, a battle between the devil on one side and the angel on the other can actually get pretty tiring. In the past, your old pattern was either to give in and scarf down a box of doughnuts or to adhere to the good angel, but with a feeling of deprivation or even anger that you had to go without while somebody else got to eat the sponge cake.

But what if there was a third voice? The voice of ego. Freud said that this part of our personality is the realistic part. It can be a mediator between the loudest voices, the id, and the superego. This is the part that says, 'You're hungry? Let's make a healthy choice.' It's the part that says, 'Mindfulness is a way of detaching from the urge of hunger.' Or it's the part that says, 'You can make healthy choices that taste better than just some raw celery.' I wonder if you could think now of some healthy choices that your ego can bring to this debate between the id and the superego. I wonder how your ego can create a plan that craves healthy choices and also doesn't simply resign to unsustainable choices like a diet.

I'll give you some time here in our session to just think, to listen to the ego, and to create your plan for making choices that are both exciting and healthy. You'll probably notice something. You'll probably notice that in your mind are visions or pictures or images of the healthy choices you can make. Or, if you take in a breath, it's as if you can practically smell the delicious choices that you can make. Or you can simply notice in your body an ability to be present with hunger without the urge to take action, and it feels pretty good.

As we continue with our session 5, 4, 3, 2, 1, each breath relaxes you even further into the experience. 3, 2, 1, 0."

Practice makes perfect. When I watch the Super Bowl on television and see the singers out there singing at half-time, they have practiced their set before they did it on television. Have you ever been to a comedy club and seen a really funny comedian? They have practiced those jokes, the timing, the speed, the tonality, hundreds of times, most likely in front of a mirror before actually delivering them on stage. A magician practices his card tricks a hundred times before he shows them to someone.

It's amazing how in counseling, hypnosis, and NLP, we don't really talk about practicing, but it is practice that makes it perfect. I'm convinced that the best way to practice is to do these things in self-hypnosis. You can take these scripts I'm giving you, put them up on your screen, and practice self-hypnosis on your desk using these same ideas.

You have probably seen clients who have panic, anxiety, fears, or phobias. The Freudian approach or the psychodynamic approach asks somebody to be an observer of their experience and create realization into their experience. In transactional analysis, we are altering our ego states so that we can change emotions. We are producing change, so we have a different end result. We have the parent role, the adult role, the child role, and the different positions of transactional analysis. Then we have our set of presuppositions, as we call it in NLP, assumptions that a transactional approach takes to the work we do with clients. I think all of these elements, these presuppositions of transactional analysis, are really important.

I have three dogs, and I don't train them by punching, hitting, or spanking them. I give them positive reinforcement. I give my dogs some steak I get on sale, dehydrate it and give it to them as dog treats. It's a lot easier to get my dogs to not jump up, not come into the house when I don't want them to, or to do what I want them to do when I give them positive reinforcement. My theory is that if it's good enough for dogs, it's good enough for people! People respond to positive reinforcement. That is the cool thing about transactional analysis. It's not an approach that's focused on the problem.

Transactional analysis assumes that people have the capacity for love. Their capacity for love may have been impacted by their traumas, distrust, and experiences, but we all have the capacity for love. We have the ability to think. This is really important in transactional analysis. All these ego states have value. People can decide their own story. In other words, we are empowered to make the changes in our lives that are essential. And so often, people do not believe that they have the ability to decide their story or their ending. People can change their stories, and all emotional difficulties can be resolved—every single one of them. It might not be resolved quickly, but it can be resolved.

I do not believe in hypnotists promising to fix everything in one session or with a five-step promise. What I do believe is that we have the ability, sometimes quickly, sometimes slowly, to change all our emotions or problems. Transactional analysis teaches us that we are going to be able to do that. By altering the ego states, we can change our emotions.

Below is a transactional analysis script including the short process I teach clients. I call it the 3, 2, 1 technique for panic, fear, or stress. It's really a great strategy.

"3, 2, 1. Take **three** breaths. You do not have to breathe in a special way. You can breathe quickly or slowly, and you can breathe deeply if you want to. It's important to just breathe and count the three breaths.

Take your **two** hands and cross them over your upper body with the left hand on the right shoulder and the right hand on the left shoulder—as if hugging yourself. And you can pat yourself gently with your hands. Spend **one** minute observing the breath."

During this minute, you're not stopping your thoughts, emotions, or feelings. You're practicing not following them and keeping your attention in the present moment. You can, of course, spend more than one minute focusing on the breath.

Or you could just sit there if you wanted to, just giving yourself a little hug that actually makes us feel good, whether somebody else is hugging us or we are hugging ourselves.

This next script is similar top havening, eye movement desensitization and reprocessing (EMDR), or slowed bilateral stimulation.

"Close your eyes and take one minute to be mindful. Pay attention to this moment. Over the next minute, set aside any regrets from yesterday, any fears of tomorrow, and stay present in this moment, paying attention to your breath and recognizing that at this moment, you are doing exactly what you need to be doing—learning, experiencing, and changing.

If you notice your mind jumping ahead into the future, bring it back to the present moment, to the breath. If you see yourself walking into the past, bring your awareness to the breath in the present moment.

With a smile on your face, 4,3,2,1, open your eyes. Now, notice your physiology. Is it different now than it was moments ago? Is your breath different? Is your heart rate different? Are your awareness, senses, and balance different now than just moments ago? It's amazing how quickly we can actually change ourselves."

You can see how this script corresponds to the graphic here of our transactional analysis understanding.

TRANSACTIONAL ANALYSIS

(The Communicator Alters the Ego-State
to Change Emotions)

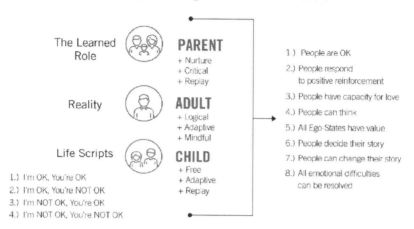

The Learned Role

PARENT
+ Nurture
+ Critical
+ Replay

Reality

ADULT
+ Logical
+ Adaptive
+ Mindful

Life Scripts

CHILD
+ Free
+ Adaptive
+ Replay

1.) I'm OK, You're OK
2.) I'm OK, You're NOT OK
3.) I'm NOT OK, You're OK
4.) I'm NOT OK, You're NOT OK

1.) People are OK
2.) People respond to positive reinforcement
3.) People have capacity for love
4.) People can think
5.) All Ego-States have value
6.) People decide their story
7.) People can change their story
8.) All emotional difficulties can be resolved

We do not need to know everything about IFS to use these scripts because these concepts may be articulated in a certain way by any of these proponents of various methods of parts therapy. We probably have both our own personal experiences with parts and our experiences in working with clients, whether we were either consciously or unconsciously working with the different parts of their personality to put this into action or use.

In internal family systems, there is also something called the six Fs. So, we have the eight Cs, and we have the six Fs:

1. Find
2. Focus
3. Flesh it out
4. Feel
5. BeFriend
6. Fear

These six Fs are important components. What's great about the six Fs in internal family systems is they can be used by any hypnotist as a process or script for any hypnosis session.

Our client wants to move from where they are now to where they want to be—their outcome. Aspects of the exiles still exist due to trauma in general, and either the managers or firefighters can assist them in moving toward their outcome. The six Fs give us a process for being able to do that.

There are three stages to the six Fs:

1. Awareness of a part: We want to have our client find the part, focus on the part, and flesh it out.
2. Our client has to decide whether this part of their personality is welcome. How do they feel toward that part?
3. Our client needs to connect with and befriend that part and deal with the fear that part has brought to them.

Below is a script using the six Fs. These are questions, prompts, and suggestions. Again, an induction and a deepener have been given to the client.

"Go ahead and close your eyes. 3,2,1,0. There is a part of you that truly wanted to be here today to learn and to experience. Find that part of you that craves knowledge, learning, and creativity. When you become aware of that part, ask yourself how you experience that part. Look inside and listen to the voices of those parts. Pay attention to your body and see where you experience that part of you that loves learning.

Now focus on the aspects of that part of you that really stand out to you. Listen to what it says. Explore that part. Observe it. Attend to it. Be with it. It is amazing how by simply doing these things, we can find, we can focus, and we can flesh out different parts of ourselves and our personalities. Sometimes those parts are unwanted. Sometimes those parts are needed, wanted, and welcomed. Ask yourself if this part where learning takes place, this part where creativity is formed, where techniques are strategized is beneficial to you? Is it wanted?

As a hypnosis counseling educator, I hear a lot of people say they can't really get in touch with that part. They feel like they are not growing in their profession. But you've come here today because this is a part you've truly wanted to be with. And so, you can ask yourself what is the best way for you to connect to that part, and what other parts of your personality can you align with this part? This part may be unique and serve a different purpose than the other parts of your personality. And then, you may have gotten this job out of necessity. Almost all of us got into this profession so that we could figure out how to help ourselves first. You can explore this part and find out if this part of you is satisfied with its job and what that part is afraid of. What would happen if it did not do its job in the same way? It is amazing how it just quickly goes through this list over the past three or four minutes, everybody here in this room with their eyes closed or even with their eyes open. It is really touching that part where learning takes place, where exploration lies, and where creativity exists.

You can probably see yourself this week in the sessions that you do. Benefit people with some of the things you've learned here in only week number one of our session. Let a smile come on your face, take a breath, pay attention to the room around you, my voice, the chair below you, and be ready in the coming week to take this handout with the six Fs of IFS and, either quickly as we have done here or as slowly as you would like, explore the different parts of your personality. So then, passionately, we can do that with care and compassion for those who have trusted us with an appointment they've made. Let a smile come on your face, opening your eyes, feeling fantastic and ready for the rest of the day."

The client will likely be relaxed and excited. It is always so amazing what the transformation can be.

CHAPTER FIVE:

Dr. Richard Nongard's Model of Parts

Having written about parts and parts therapy and different therapists and theorists, you will appreciate that some people have come up with creative names for the parts. For example, Schwartz had exiles, firefighters, and managers. Others have conceptualized these parts with various names. I prefer to simply ask my client what they call that part rather than give them a label from my perspective or from my vantage point. But the way I conceptualize parts and the different parts that we work with, you will see integrate into a system. By integrating it into a system, we can create interventions, hypnotic suggestions—both indirect and direct suggestions—as well as truly helpful processes. In my conceptualization of parts, I do not have cute names for each of these.

It is important to recognize that below I discuss five parts. Each one of these parts has a core concept behind it. My conceptualization of parts begins with the first part, our physical self.

Physical

One of the things I have noticed in many different models of parts therapy is that they almost always neglect the physical component of who we are. This physical aspect, I think, is inseparable from the spiritual aspect or from the psychological aspect. I think the mind, the body, and the spirit are really on a continuum and an extension of each other. I like to conceptualize parts therapy, recognizing that the physical aspect is that parts of us are actual literal parts.

This is important because your clients will say, "A part of me hurts." This could be hurt from emotional pain, a medical issue, a temporary experience they are having, or an ongoing chronic problem. As hypnotists, we know that the most well-researched use of hypnosis is a first-line intervention. It is a helpful tool for physical conditions, psychological and emotional conditions, behavioral change, peak performance, and helping a person to really engage the variety of different solutions in their life. Probably the most well-researched application or use of hypnosis is in hypnotic pain control. Your client will have a part of them that's in pain, either chronic pain, acute pain, or episodic pain. We are affected emotionally by our physical condition. I can only function emotionally as well as I can function physically.

Years ago, I used to work out at a gym with a personal trainer. The gym had a relationship with a rehabilitation hospital that was directly next door. Patients would be in the gym doing some rehab work and strength training, etc. One day, I watched a man who was probably 400 to 450 pounds on the treadmill, walking very, very slowly, and the trainer was standing next to him. I didn't know what was really going on, but I realized that the trainer had just done a therapy session with the man. But rather than talking about making change, that trainer had actually engaged in change with the client.

I thought to myself, *instead of being in my office talking about these things, what if I put a treadmill in my office?* I bought a treadmill and put it in my office. I would have some of my clients walk on the treadmill, putting into action their physical part as we discussed and found solutions for the emotional problems they brought to my office. It was probably one of the biggest changes I made. That was in 2005. I went on from there and got certified as a personal trainer, not so I could work as a trainer but because I realized that I didn't know what I needed to know about the relationship between physical wellness and emotional health. I was much more aware of that afterward.

Associated

Anyone familiar with NLP knows that an associated state is one where a person is actively participating. This is their present experience. They are associated into an emotion, a resource state, an experience, or an awareness. When I conceptualize the part of us that is associated, I'm conceptualizing the part that is present, engaged, fighting off a problem, or implementing a solution. The associated parts are those that, if we want to use Freud's model of the conscious and unconscious mind, are at the top of our awareness level. We have associated parts, and these are our primary. These are front and center. One could be, from a personality perspective, our guardian. It could be guarding us with positive coping strategies or unhealthy coping strategies, but it is still serving that purpose because it is always on guard.

Repressed

This is different from repressed memory. There has been a lot of misinformation about repressed memory. The fact of the matter is that, with many of my clients, their problem isn't that they can't remember their trauma. Their problem is that they are associated into it, and they are living their trauma.

Repressed parts are the attributes or the characteristics of our personality. These are the members of our personalities that, unlike the associated parts, are not at the forefront. They're in the background, and we can tap into them at any time, but it's not our first inclination. It's not our first response. They're often second to the scene. Each one of us has parts that are repressed or held back.

They can be held back for several different reasons. It could be that they are not strong yet. One of our goals in therapy is to strengthen these parts. It could be that a part is consumed with fear. Because it is consumed with fear, it stays in the background and lets another part take the lead and be associated in that moment. We all have these repressed parts.

Team

These are the helpers. In the context of IFS, these are the firefighters. These are the parts of us that say, "Hey, you need to come to the front," or "You need to step to the back," or "You need to take care of your physical self so that we can solve this problem in front of us." These team members are the parts of our personality that play a role in integrating and bringing these different parts together.

Symbolic Self

If you want to put it in the context of Freud, this could be the superego. This is where the moralistic, spiritual, religious, and legalistic parts are. There are many elements of this symbolic self. This is the person who finds meaning in ritual.

When we think of ritual, we think of an orthodox priest with incense and smoke. We think of joss sticks in the Buddhist temple and incense burning. We think of a rosary bead or prayers. Those are all rituals that can be a part of the symbolic self. People engage in habit, and habit is a ritual. Habit lies in the part of us that is symbolic. We compulsively smoke cigarettes, bite our fingernails, and crack our knuckles. Because they are symbolic for us, these habits that we have serve a purpose for us even though they do not really serve a purpose in the grand scheme of things. We have attached a meaning to them that serves our purposes.

We have these five primary parts. You will notice they spell out an acronym so you can easily remember it.

In the graphic, you can see I have structured it like a family tree. These are the parts of us that are primary, and each part has children—if you want to use this metaphor analogy. People are complex. There are probably three or more parts of our physical self, associated parts, repressed parts, our team players, and our symbolic selves.

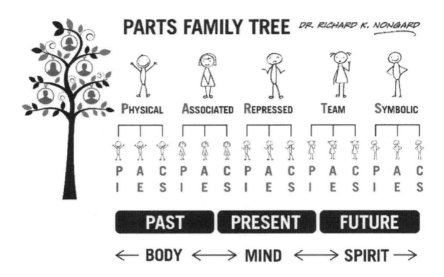

On the graphic, you will notice the text P-A-C, P-A-C, P-A-C, P-A-C, and I-E-S, I-E-S, I-E-S. (Parent-Adult-Child, and Id-Ego-Superego)

We could conceptualize this model in conjunction with other models. One of the things I want to emphasize to you is that everything works together. If you were going to write a book about me, you could say that one of the presuppositions of Richard Nongard is that everything works together no matter how chaotic it may seem. We can take my conceptualization—physical, associated, repressed, team, symbolic— and we can look at the parts of each one of these parts.

One of these parts is perhaps the parent, the adult, and the child. One of these associated parts is the sentry—the guardian. Rather than coming up with labels for the parts, I ask my clients, "What do you call that part?" I think that's important. That can be revealing and better than the approach of telling them what the parts are named. Your clients will come up with a name for their parts. It might be an actual name, or they'll come up with all kinds of different labels for it.

Let's look at the repressed part. This could be the part of me that has shame. I'm going to call this part Shane. Shane is always there no matter where I go, and Shane is no fun. Shane is always telling me that I shouldn't do this or I can't do that. The reason why is that it would be embarrassing or humiliating. That would be the worst thing ever.

I listen to Shane way too much rather than listening to another part of me. That part is one of the team players. I call him Coach B. Coach B is one of the team players who is always telling me, "Hey. You need to have Shane move up to the frontline in the game and play defense."

We can have a child, a parent, and an adult for each of these different parts of the bigger part, or back to Freud's conceptualization, we can have an id, an ego, and a superego. You can't go wrong because one of the presuppositions of hypnosis is that clients will attach meaning to those ideas that are most important. Sometimes they'll attach meanings to the sessions you do, and they can be different to what you thought about or what you came up with.

Rather than using the parent, adult, child, or the id, the ego, and the superego, I almost always look at the parts of our parts in the context of the past me, the present me, and the future me. My goal in the therapy I do is to move our past into the present and our future into the present. The reason why is simple. Much of our therapeutic approach—based on Sigmund Freud—is to go back and revisit the past. And no matter how much time we spend on the past, the reality is we cannot change it. But we have to recognize the past. The past brought us to where we are today. Having an understanding of the past is important.

The initial sensitizing event, the ISE, is a useful relapse prevention tool. But I don't believe it's a very useful tool to help people make a change.

I think we can help people make change without ever knowing why we do the things that we do. Most of my clients' problems are that they are either stuck in the past. They are not living in the present moment. They have regrets and fears. They have many different parts to them that they've carried from the past. And so, I conceptualize these parts as the parts of the past and ask the question, "How, in therapy, can we move forward into the present?"

Some of my clients are not stuck in the past with regret, remorse, or self-flagellation but are often stuck in the future. These are my anxiety, panic, and fear-based clients. "What if . . . ?" They can't live in the moment because a part of them is always projecting into the future. My predominant approach, whether therapy, counseling, or any coaching strategy, is to help people move these parts to the present moment so all these parts together can be here and now.

If all these parts are here and now and they are resources to me, I can solve just about anything. I can do things with all my parts that I can't do with just one part. For example, if my car were to run out of gas. There's a gas station about six blocks from where I'm standing in my driveway. I can't push it down the part of my street, and then onto the busy main road, and then get it across the median strip and over to the gas station. I can't do that by myself. Let's imagine there are twenty or more of us, and we all get behind my car. Can we push it six blocks to the gas station? We can do that together. We can do things together that we can't do alone.

This is why I find when we get all these parts together in the present moment, using contextual approaches, acceptance and commitment therapy, mindfulness-based stress reduction, solution-focused brief therapy, cognitive behavioral therapy, and other approaches that focus on the present rather than resolving the past, they can all function together in a resource state that can make the possibilities for clients' experiences truly unlimited.

There's something else I want you to notice about this conceptualization of parts and parts therapy. I want you to notice that what we really have here is body, mind, and spirit, the metaphysical aspects of our experiences. This is a holistic understanding—body, mind, and spirit.

When we talk about doing holistic therapy, where we see a person not as an isolated problem or an isolated part but as a whole, we can do great things with those clients from a praxeological perspective. This model of parts work in hypnosis is a model that, I think, we can explore and that we can build on to truly find the benefit for our clients.

You will discover it is a powerful process that we can use with just about any client who comes into our office or that we meet with on Zoom to help them live their best life. That's really the promise of hypnosis. Professional hypnosis promises that when your clients learn hypnosis, their problems will begin to disappear when they come to see you. They discover a new freedom—a new way of managing life. They discover new opportunities they didn't know about before. By having this model as a foundation, we can then take our other learnings from IFS, transactional analysis, Sigmund Freud, and any other understanding of parts work and do great things with the clients we work with.

CHAPTER SIX:

Trauma and Adverse Childhood Experiences

We have been focusing on different overviews of systems, understandings, and ways of viewing parts therapy, ego states, and how all these things come together. In this chapter, I want to move on to some conceptualizations of how we can solve problems and show you some individual techniques.

Most people come to parts work because they are interested in helping people to resolve, deal with, understand, or in some way manage their experiences with trauma, adverse childhood experiences, and traumatically stressful events that they've experienced. For most of the parts work that we are talking about, therapists are drawn to the idea that this is a truly useful strategy in helping people with these experiences.

Trauma can come in a lot of different forms. It can come in the form of something that somebody does to us. It can be an internal issue. It can be something physical, and it can be something emotional. It can occur in the context of families, communities, and the world around us. Many people have a lot of different traumas, which can be anything ranging from a one-time event like a car accident to an ongoing event like a chronic illness or disease that a person has.

Let's create a big umbrella for the word "trauma" and put many things under it. This is important because we don't want to exclude people from being able to take advantage of the tools that parts therapy and ego states therapy give us to help people experience better lives. I'd rather err on the side of making the tent too big than on the side of making the tent too small.

ACEs

Adverse childhood experiences is something I talked about in my TEDx talk. If you have never watched it, you can simply go to nongardtedx.com, and that will redirect you over to the YouTube video from TEDx of my presentation. There are ten adverse childhood experiences. There are actually a lot more than that, but ten that researchers have called ACEs.

The problem with ACEs is that, unlike in Las Vegas, the more ACEs you are dealt with, the worse the outcomes are for your later life—the more learning problems, vocational problems, incarceration rates, etc. Adverse childhood experiences include physical abuse, sexual abuse, and verbal abuse. It includes emotional neglect. It includes a parent who may be incarcerated, a mentally ill mother, and losing a parent through death or divorce. These are the most common and traumatic adverse childhood experiences that correlate to predictors of problems that adults have in life.

Why would it be true that these experiences correlate to a greater number, but not always, of negative or unhealthy outcomes? Well, the reason is simple. We put it in the context of parts therapy. Due to these adverse childhood experiences, parts of us do not have the opportunity to develop fully and healthily. At the same time, other parts of us might emerge to help us in our childhood to be able to solve a problem with a child's understanding of the experiences. But when that same strategy is mapped over into the adult world, it is ineffective and doesn't work.

I am a present-minded therapist. I focus on the now. I practice mindfulness. I am far more interested in today than yesterday or the future. But we cannot lose sight of the fact that the past brought us to exactly where we are. I can guarantee you—watch my TEDx talk— that if it hadn't been for the ACEs that I've been dealt with, I probably wouldn't be here today teaching and working with individuals. I'd probably have an entirely different career than a therapist or professional hypnotist.

Traumatic Stress

I'm focusing here on PTSD as it is diagnosed in the recently released DSM-5-TR. These are stresses where the response to a stressful event is causing them significant difficulty in important areas of life, well past the time period where we would normally expect the impact of that traumatic experience to cause them problems in life.

We can even expand the diagnosis. I have never been a fan of the terms PTSD or post-traumatic stress disorder. I think it's entirely rational that people experience difficulty adjusting to a new life after difficult traumas. I don't really like that term disorder, preferring just to call it post-traumatic stress. But different people experience different outcomes to the experiences they've had. I gave this example when I talked about post-traumatic stress.

The firefighters who went into the World Trade Center on September 11th, 2001, rode there in the same trucks together. They worked in the same fire stations together. They entered the buildings, and some of them perished. Some of them were injured. Some heroically saved other people's lives both in the building and on the ground and emerged on the other side of this traumatic stress—something that they've never experienced before.

Some of those firefighters developed significant impairments that affected their families, communities, work, psychological states and included problems ranging from suicides to addictions to divorces.

Others came from that exact same experience, and rather than manifesting these sets of outcomes, they manifested a different set of outcomes. Following that situation, many of them emerged on the other side, probably far better than I would have in that particular situation. They became leaders in their community and worked with others who weren't as fortunate as they were, yet they also experienced the same traumatic stress. We have to recognize that whether the outcome received from traumatic stress is something we would be amazed by or something we see as tragic, the event was still a traumatic stressor. Those traumatic stressors affect us on a physical level, emotional, spiritual, and social level.

Trauma and the Brain

There are a couple of concepts related to the development of trauma, the experience of trauma, and the development of outcomes. The top part of our brain—the front part of our brain—is the logical part of the brain, the thinking part of the brain. This is the neocortex. This is where language is processed and where higher thinking and order occur. This emerges as we go through the developmental stages of life and fully develop into late adolescents and early adulthood.

At the center of our brain, we have the mammalian brain. This is the emotional context of the brain where our feelings, joys, and pain exist.

Then we have the amygdala—the reptile brain—the oldest part of the brain. In evolutionary biology, we started with a smaller brain, and it kept getting bigger as we essentially kept getting smarter. But this part of the brain controls breathing, respiration, physical awareness, reproduction, sexual urges, and everything that provides for the survival of the fittest. It is the most protected part of the brain.

Here's what happens when people experience trauma. Adverse childhood experiences and traumatic stressors in our lives affect us physically first. It threatens us. This is the definition of trauma— something that is a real threat to our existence, our experience. It speaks to the old brain, to the amygdala. It speaks to this unconscious part of us, physically affecting us. I've mentioned before the book *The Body Keeps the Score*. This book helps us understand how trauma, adverse childhood experiences, and traumatic stressors are first experienced physically.

In the conceptualization of parts therapy, the first part was physical. It cannot be overlooked as we try to address the problems of trauma, ACEs, and traumatic stress. There are two primary approaches to helping clients who have experienced trauma in the world of therapy.

The Top-Down Approach

The top-down approach actually starts at the top of the brain. This is cognitive-behavioral therapy. In hypnosis, this is a direct suggestion. These are therapists who teach a person to change their thinking to change their lives. Top-down therapists presume that when we think differently, we feel differently. When we feel different, we act differently. This may be true.

As a therapist, I first learned about cognitive behavioral therapy in grad school, and it has been a predominant approach of mine. In my work with clients in hypnosis, cognitive behavioral therapy has been a tremendous resource for me. It is a great source of direct suggestions. In his book, *Rational Emotive Behavior Therapy*, Albert Ellis really kicked off our awareness in 1970 of the efficacy of cognitive-behavioral therapy, which is, by the way, an evidence-based approach and has lots of research behind it. Ellis devoted two chapters to explaining how he uses hypnosis as a tool to deliver counters to cognitive errors in what are commonly known as rational emotive behavior therapy and cognitive-behavioral therapy.

Two pioneers of the field with largely the same concepts overlapped. Aaron Beck called it cognitive behavioral therapy. Albert Ellis called it rational emotive behavior therapy. People are usually trained in the ideas and methods of both because they are really dealt with together.

In fact, over the last forty or fifty years since they published their books, there has been a tremendous amount of research and other researchers' teaching methods.

One of my favorite books is Dr. Bruce Eimer's *Brief Cognitive Hypnosis*. He wrote it with Jordan Zarren, a social worker in Florida. This book really looks closely at these top-down approaches. Even though a top-down approach starts with the top part of the brain and goes down to the old brain, these approaches are periodically validated. They work, and they're highly effective. They're used by therapists and hypnotists around the country today.

The Bottom-Up Approach

This has fast become my favorite approach to dealing with trauma, adverse childhood experiences, and post-traumatic stress because it starts with the body. It really starts at the bottom, and it goes up to create experiences, changes, emotional resource states, changes in thinking and logic, and self-talk in a language. I was really lucky in my training. I was trained in grad school in cognitive-behavioral therapy, but my first practicum supervisor, Dean P. Montgomery, Ph.D., trained me in Ericksonian hypnosis. He was a student of Milton Erickson. He taught me the methods of Ericksonian hypnosis, and I fell in love with hypnotherapy.

As a twenty-two-year-old therapist in grad school, I had just finished going through a difficult adolescence and childhood packed with adverse childhood experiences, traumas, and post-traumatic stress. Sitting in the Dean's office, as he taught me Ericksonian hypnosis and I experienced hypnosis, it was the first time that my body felt still. My attention deficit disorder was through the roof. My anxiety would cause me to shake papers and books, and my body kept score. It was holding the residuals of my own traumas. I did not realize it at that time. Dean taught me to take a breath and relax, to pay attention to the muscles in my body, and to notice the difference between tension and relaxation. It was the first time anyone taught me to address the physical part of myself. The result has been magnificent.

For much of my twenties and early and mid-thirties, I spent most of my time helping other people and working with people. I also spent a lot of my time still wrestling with some of my own traumas and difficulties. The physical effects caused health problems in a thirty-something-year-old man that probably shouldn't have been experienced until sixty or more in age. These manifested in several different areas, and now I understand why.

I also understand that hypnosis is a tremendous solution because hypnosis starts with the body most of the time. It does not start with the thought. It starts with paying attention to the breath. It starts with exhaling. It starts with feeling the chair below your fingertips and paying attention to the air in the room around you, and just being present. It involves scanning the body, noticing any parts of the body where tension is being held, and letting that tension go. Hypnosis is a bottom-up approach. It begins with the body and moves toward emotions, logic, language, cognitive-behavioral hypnosis, direct suggestions, etc., which is probably why I was drawn to it, and why it has been so important to me for so many years.

For you and the clients you work with, I want you to keep in mind that the approaches of hypnosis that focus on therapeutic relaxation are important. I have often heard hypnotists say, "Well, I would never do relax therapy or muscle relaxation." That just bores them in hypnosis, which Milton Erickson said was a very effective way of going into hypnosis. But hypnosis is often a bottom-up approach. When we are dealing with people who are traumatically wounded, we often have to start with the body before we can deal with the emotional content and before we can deal with the thought patterns, self-talk, and the language of self-care.

CHAPTER SEVEN:

Focusing Script

Eugene Gendlin was a philosopher and psychotherapist. He developed an important approach called focusing. In this chapter, I'll be sharing some interventions and ideas related to Gendlin's approach to focusing.

What is one of the ways that we can begin the hypnotic session with the bottom-up approach? There are six steps, principles, or keys in Gendlin's ideas. Gendlin never used the word hypnosis nor talked about this as a hypnotic method. But I think he'll recognize that many people who have come up with some great ideas have articulated those ideas, and as hypnotists, we recognize that these are really hypnotic ideas.

This is an approach that I have certainly worked on with my clients with ACEs, traumatic stress, and trauma because it begins by looking at the P part. That is the physical part of the approach in this experience. All the different approaches and theories have their own different ideals, but really they blend together. I think this approach blends together with *The Body Keeps the Score* and with some of the ideas that Carl Jung articulated related to personality and even Sigmund Freud.

The six steps are:

1. Clearing a space
2. Felt sense
3. Handle
4. Resonating
5. Asking
6. Receiving

These are the steps in the process that Gendlin gave us for focusing as a strategy that looks at the physical part. I want you to recognize that in our hypnosis sessions, I can do hypnosis in one of two ways. I can sit my client in a chair, put headphones on them, speak to them through a microphone, and deliver an induction, deepener, indirect, direct, posthypnotic, reorientation, and ratification. I can do what we often think of as a start-to-finish hypnosis session.

But as most of you know, even if we do a twenty, thirty, or forty-minute session with a client, we will be spending additional time with that client before the pretalk and often after the session. In these conversations with the client, we are still doing hypnosis. We are still using conversational hypnosis. We can literally use Gendlin's process as a hypnosis script for a formal hypnosis process. And we can also use it conversationally and experientially with someone.

Both ways are great ways of helping and working with clients.

I will guide you through the process, as once again, I find that when we experience something positively, we can passionately share it with other people.

As you pay attention to this chapter, bring yourself to a resourceful state of learning, of open-mindedness, and one that is beneficial to you.

Adaption of Gendlin's ideas. The Focusing Script:

"Step 1

Note the feeling of your body, both the outside of your body as well as the inside of your body. You are not looking for anything specific that I want you to find. Rather, you are looking inside your own body and experiences, and you are noting that which is important to you.

When you note something of importance, it is important that you do not associate into it and become that thing. Just become aware of it. Now, note the other places in your body, both within the body and on the outside of your body. Perhaps it is an itch. Perhaps it is hunger. Perhaps it is an ache inside a muscle, inside your heart, or inside your mind. Perhaps it is some other experience that you have. Perhaps it is a feeling of coolness or of comfort. You are just noting the body and whatever else you note in the body. And in this first step, clearing a space, what we are really doing is becoming aware of our experience from our physical perspective, that physical part of us.

Step 2

In the felt sense step, you are going to choose an awareness that you have now after completing Step 1. Again, I am going to ask you to keep some space between you and that part. As you keep some space between you and that part, do not allow yourself to associate into that part and become that part. But sense what all the problems that you've been carrying feel like in that part. What is amazing is that simply by asking you to sense what all those problems you've been carrying feel like in that part, you immediately and intuitively understand what that means, which gives you the ability in your own mind's eye to sense all those problems.

Step 3

Now we are going to really understand this part of our body that we sense, and what the problem feels like and all of that in our body." (If you have any NLP training, this will come in handy as we deal with

55

submodalities.) "What is the quality of that problem? Do you experience it? Can you conceptualize it as a word? As an image? As an experience? Is it far? Is it near? Is it outside your body even though you know it is inside your body? Is it something that is inside your body that stays inside your body? Is it something that has a noise? Is that noise far or near? Is it loud or quiet? How does it speak to you?" (Each one of us is going to explore this in different ways. By exploring, and especially with the ideas of the NLP submodalities, we get a handle on the problem and what it feels like, and we can sense all that.)

Step 4

Here we go back and forth between our awareness, our felt sense, and that image or word or experience that we just created. Allow yourself to experience going back and forth between the word, image, or experience that you associate with this recognition and your awareness or part of your body that holds this problem and what it feels like. It's pretty amazing the way we are able to do these things as we focus, often on a part which hasn't had the opportunity to be fully present in our life.

Step 5

This is asking what is it about that part that gives the quality or the characteristic of the problem. There are really two parts to step five. The first is to be with that problem and attend to it and ask, "What is this sense or awareness?" The second is that by returning awareness to the body, you can ask again, "What is it about this part that makes the experience or the quality of this word or this image?" Allow yourself in your own mind and in your own recognition to develop insight and awareness.

Step 6

Even though I only did a brief exercise with you, notice how your experience has shifted. The shift may be profound, and perhaps you will notice it now or in a while. Perhaps the shift is just in the way you are breathing, your respiration, your heart rate. Another way is that you may notice how your muscles feel. Embrace that shift if it is present. Also, embrace the process even if you do not notice a shift. The shift may come later, and it may require more work. The shift may have been something that was accomplished by simply allowing yourself to pay attention to that part for the very first time.

Take a deep breath. Let a smile come to your face. Pay attention to the air in the room around you. Pay attention to my voice. Pay attention to the floor below you. Open your eyes. Open your eyes, having gone through each of these six processes of focusing. This is a very grounded and grounding exercise, like breathing and body scan meditations from yoga and other disciplines, in the physical components of our parts and our experiences."

My hope is that by sharing this and letting you go through an abbreviated process, you found personal benefit and understood some ideas that can help you with the clients that you work with and experience success at every level in the future.

CHAPTER EIGHT:

Using Scripts in Parts Work

Let's talk about scripts briefly because people pontificate all the time about why they would never use a hypnosis script. Most of the hypnotists I know use hypnosis scripts. They've done the process so many times that it's committed to memory. Even though they don't have a piece of paper in front of them, they're largely using a script. I could say, for example, I've done so many stop smoking sessions I'd never use a script. But if you were to watch me do a stop smoking session with my client, it would probably be very similar to what I did with my clients a year ago, three years ago, and five years ago. Sure, there are some individual differences in adaptations. We should do that with any hypnosis script. But the reality is that I'm still using a script. It's just a script that I have committed to memory.

I have no problem bringing a script to sessions, even scripts on a piece of paper. I wrote a few script books that you might be interested in:

Expert Hypnosis Scripts for the Professional Hypnotist

Dr. Richard Nongard's Big Book of Hypnosis Scripts

Magic Words in Hypnosis: The Sourcebook of Hypnosis Patter and Scripts and How to Overcome Hypnotic Difficulties

Inductions and Deepeners: Styles and Approaches for Effective Hypnosis

The Self-Hypnosis Solution: Step-by-Step Methods and Scripts to Create Profound Change and Lifelong Results

I would never go into a session and just read a hypnosis script. Nor should you ever go into a session after having read a script that day. That would probably be a lousy hypnosis session. What you should do, though, is familiarize yourself with hypnosis scripts that other people have written. Just familiarize yourself with scripts that other people write. You should have them as a resource. And you should write your own. You should be able to just use a script from memory when you are very familiar with it. After all, you've read it multiple times.

Before you ever use a script, you should be able to easily change the script on the fly. You should easily adapt what is written on the paper to what your clients need is in front of you. This is a responsible use of scripts. The reason why I like to use scripts is simple. When I opened the Tulsa Hypnosis Center, I was trying to build a big practice. I packed up my schedule and hired another hypnotist. I'd see up to eight clients in a day. My associate would probably see up to eight clients in a day. It was impossible for me to remember every single thing about every single client. And so, when I share a script with my clients, I might say as part of my pre-talk, "You might hear me flip through the pages of some books or even rustle some papers. The reason why is simple. I have written some notes and have some things to share with you today to make sure that I cover everything important to you." And now, I guess I have just normalized paper, scripts, and books in the middle of the session.

One of my favorite scripts of all time comes from Chapter 30 of Herman Melville's book, *Moby-Dick*. It is the shortest chapter in the book. It is about four or five paragraphs long. This is where Captain Ahab quits smoking. Captain Ahab takes his pipe and sits on a stool made of narwhal tusks. "How now," he soliloquized at last, withdrawing the tube, 'this smoking no longer soothes . . . I'll smoke no more.' He tossed the still lighted pipe into the sea. The fire hissed in the waves; the same instant the ship shot by the bubble the sinking pipe made."

It's a great story, and I share it with many smokers. Here is the entire chapter 30, titled *The Pipe*.

CHAPTER 30. The Pipe.

When Stubb had departed, Ahab stood for a while leaning over the bulwarks; and then, as had been usual with him of late, calling a sailor of the watch, he sent him below for his ivory stool, and also his pipe. Lighting the pipe at the binnacle lamp and planting the stool on the weather side of the deck, he sat and smoked.

In old Norse times, the thrones of the sea-loving Danish kings were fabricated, saith tradition, of the tusks of the narwhale. How could one look at Ahab then, seated on that tripod of bones, without bethinking him of the royalty it symbolized? For a Khan of the plank, and a king of the sea, and a great lord of Leviathans was Ahab. Some moments passed, during which the thick vapor came from his mouth in quick and constant puffs, which blew back again into his face.

"How now," he soliloquized at last, withdrawing the tube, "this smoking no longer soothes. Oh, my pipe! hard must it go with me if thy charm be gone! Here have I been unconsciously toiling, not pleasuring—aye, and ignorantly smoking to windward all the while; to windward, and with such nervous whiffs, as if, like the dying whale, my final jets were the strongest and fullest of trouble. What business have I with this pipe? This thing that is meant for sereneness, to send up mild white vapors among mild white hairs, not among torn iron-grey locks like mine. I'll smoke no more—"

He tossed the still lighted pipe into the sea. The fire hissed in the waves; the same instant the ship shot by the bubble the sinking pipe made. With slouched hat, Ahab lurchingly paced the planks.

It's perfectly okay to use scripts. Some people get the idea that a good hypnotist would never use a script. I think a good hypnotist is well-prepared, and part of the preparation is having some notes.

John Cerbone wrote a great book called *Hypnotic Scripts That Work*, and it's one of my favorite hypnosis script books. John and I have different styles of communication. On one page is a wall of text with no paragraphs and no punctuation. There is just free-flowing rambling thought. Those of you who know John Cerbone know that this very much matches up with his personality.

Using scripts from other people is perfectly okay in our client sessions. But we want to make sure we are very familiar with them long before we actually enter into a session with them.

In Chapter 5, I shared my model or the conceptualization that I have of parts therapy. Take a look at this acronym for PARTS below.

Physical
Associated
Repressed
Team
Symbolic

The physical part of us, the associated part, the repressed part, the team part, and the symbolic part of us.

Each of us brings our own personality traits and our own parts when we conduct sessions with clients. The chart's value that I created is a holistic representation of parts therapy. That's how I've generally approached parts therapy. Every teacher of parts therapy will have their own approach. You already have the ideas of Gordon Emmerson,

Charles Tebbetts, Sigmund Freud, and Carl Jung in terms of personality temperament and personality traits—all different parts.

The chart I created is a combination of all the different learnings that I've put together to make sense for the clients I work with and for me.

Physical

Sometimes parts have names. Your client will be clear on what the name is. Many trainers in parts therapy ascribe names to the different parts, but I believe it's important that everybody represents their parts in their own way.

The label of firefighter being ascribed to a part is an example of something I'm uncomfortable doing. It could mean that this part only comes when there is a fire. Meaning is attached to it, but it's not a meaning that's resourceful to me. The meaning of that particular label was resourceful for the work the individual was doing when they came up with that label. But it might not be to somebody else. Somebody else might have their own unique experiences. My father was a firefighter. I spent my entire childhood in the back of the car, and he would throw the emergency light on and head off to fire with me in the back seat. Some of you have watched my TEDx Talk. There are issues from early childhood development. I'm just not sure that I want firefighters coming to my rescue.

I prefer not to name these parts and let clients tell me their parts' names. Sometimes a client might say, "I don't have a clue what the name is. Does it matter?" No, it doesn't matter. They actually don't need a name. I prefer descriptors for parts. I like descriptors that are very generic or are easily accepted. Have you ever used visualization in hypnosis?

My favorite visualization is a clear blue sky with a single white, puffy cloud floating lazily and leisurely through the sky towards the horizon, becoming smaller and smaller. A place you have been before, a place you'd like to go to, or a place of your own creation. This is a very non-threatening visualization.

Have you been to a place that was beautiful? Or is there a beautiful place you'd like to go to? Or can you create a mental image of what a beautiful place might be? That is achievable. Just a very basic visualization, even clients who have difficulty visualizing can usually make it through visualization with a single white, puffy cloud.

That is why we have the physical, associated, repressed, team, and symbolic parts because they are broad categories rather than the labels, unlike firefighter, which is very specific.

Associated

How about the parts of our personality that are associated, that are there, that are kind of at the tip of our personality?

Associated parts could include kindness, creativity, risk-taker, leader, peacemaker, etc.

Perhaps if you are a kind person and when people meet you, they say, "Oh, I just love Michelle. She's so kind," because that kind part is a part that leads your personality, actions, your interactions, probably even your physical traits. You have a smile on your face. That is a great example of an associated part.

Repressed

Let's talk about some of the repressed parts. Some of the parts of you that are hidden. Maybe even the parts of you that are hidden from the people who are closest to you. The parts of us that we are least likely to bring forward in any situation.

Some repressed parts are shame, controller, encourager, collaborator, etc.

Shame is a great one. John Bradshaw has a great video on YouTube from 1982 on shame and addiction that he did for Public Broadcasting Service (PBS).

Often, shame is repressed, and it is hidden behind humor, criticism, depression, and so many other things. Acknowledging that part can go a long way to helping us heal. Bradshaw's book is *Healing the Shame That Binds You.*

Team

These are the parts that come to assist other parts. This is the part that provides compassion to self-judgement, or strength when another part needs to step back.

Symbolic

Perhaps there is a peacemaker that is a part of the symbolic role that believes that peace has a moral value or attribute and that we should live in peace, like Mahatma Gandhi. But there is a part of us that is a peacemaker because it can't stand conflict. We might have two different parts of us that have that same label. The symbolic part could be the religious part. A lot of people develop religious habits to help them really understand their symbolic needs and their symbolic parts.

Back in the day, people would check into addiction treatment and have a mustache or a beard. The first thing they would have to do was shave that off. They would have to shave it off because they wanted them to change their identity, the physical masks that they were wearing. That was uncomfortable for a lot of people. They don't do that anymore because it wouldn't necessarily be considered ethical or an effective treatment mode. But it was interesting that it was done, and the purpose was to change the symbolic representation that was manifesting in an outward appearance.

A part of this symbolic self could be the teen that identifies as being a jock or a prep or a goth or whatever else teens are doing nowadays.

Up-and-coming teenager Cindy is twelve. She very much identifies as a basketball player wearing her Michael Jordan jerseys. Her parents had to buy her a $300 pair of sneakers, so she could be a basketball player. She is that basketball star and wears that outwardly. That's symbolism.

If you have studied anti-union psychology, you will see the symbolic self, the archetypes, and those ideas of the healer. Those of you who have studied the anagram are aware that it's interesting because those are all archetypes as well. They fit within the symbolic self.

I remember when I was an adolescent, I had an identity crisis, and I thought to myself, *Who am I?* And then I realized I'm Richard Nongard, and I got to define what that means. Over the years, I've paid a lot of attention to who I am. Some of these things I have liked, and some of these things I have not liked. For example, there's a part of me that has absolutely no ability to be fashionable or well-dressed.

My wife is very fashionable and always looks her best. I don't have that ability. I can buy a $150 shirt and make it look like it came from a used clothing store. It doesn't matter how much or how little I spend on clothes; I'm always the worst-dressed guy in the room.

And so, in developing my identity, I had to embrace that part of me that was just a little weird when it came to the way I looked. Now it's my trademark. I quit trying to wear a tie. My wife tried to get me to change, and I decided, "You know what? I'm just going to embrace it." I'm the guy who wears $20 Bass Pro Shops cargo pants with a $570 Gucci hat. The reason why is that I can't figure out how to coordinate this stuff.

We have these different parts of ourselves. Our clients come to us, and they don't know who they are. I think it's a good exercise to help our clients explore the parts of their personalities.

The physical part could be a physical awareness—a pain or a non-pain. It could be an attribute or an extension of us that is physical. It could be something temporary or permanent. But just like we scan our bodies as in yoga for a body scan meditation, we can scan our bodies and become aware of our bodies. We can literally do a parts scan and scan the parts of our personalities.

I have created a script for you below. It includes an induction and a deepener and goes through each of these five parts and asks us to identify the other parts within those parts because it includes the parts family tree. One of my favorite words in a hypnosis script is "notice." One of my other favorite words in the hypnosis script is "experience." Both words allow a person to interpret them in a way that is meaningful to them.

"Scan your body. Look for the parts of your body that are represented in this moment. Pay attention to your body. Notice things you have not noticed before."

Look at the associated elements of our parts. We probably have more than one component. For example, if it's extroversion, we might have extroversion and other parts of our associated personality. It could be leadership, autonomy, or perseverance. Guiding a person through this process with each of these five parts can give them a chance to really understand themselves. No one's probably going to make an appointment with you and say, "Hi. I'd like to schedule an appointment for parts therapy, so I can check out the different parts."

But when we're working with clients, we might help them become aware of their parts to help move them to a level of peak performance or to a greater state.

"By noticing the body, the parts of your body, you can bring awareness to the present. Noticing parts that need attention and the parts that give us ability. Some of our physical parts give us ability. In your current awareness, we call these associated parts—the parts not only in our body that we are aware of, but the personal personality or present state that we are aware of, the repressed parts or the parts of us that are hidden. Perhaps with your conscious mind, you know that they exist, or you have reserved paying attention to them for certain moments. On the other hand, some of these parts might be deeply hidden. Parts that bring joy or parts that bring pain—notice these parts. They can become quite clear when we just take a moment in hypnosis to pay attention to the parts. Perhaps they remain clouded or hidden, only knowing that they are present rather than feeling their presence."

This is a line in the script I want you to pay attention to:

"They might become quite clear when you pay attention to these parts. They may remain clouded or hidden, only knowing that they are present rather than feeling their presence."

This gives a client permission to experience it in the way that I hope they do. In other words, I never want to put pressure on a client. If I was doing autogenic training and I said,

"Just think of the word warmth. Pay attention to the word warmth. Let your hands feel warmth. Think of the word heavy. Let your hands feel a sense of heaviness."

I want my clients to have warm and heavy hands when I throw in these lines and become aware or notice a sensation of warmth at any level or heaviness in any way. I want to give my client the freedom to experience and become aware of these things in a way that they are comfortable with within the moment, recognizing that we are probably going to grow further.

"You can identify these parts, choosing to feel them, hear them, acknowledge them, or experience them. You can choose to let them remain ambiguous, simply knowing that you have acknowledged these parts."

I'm a firm believer that we should let clients bring to therapy whatever they are ready to deal with. I was trained early on in gestalt therapy—

the old substance abuse treatment model. Put them on the hot seat and break through that denial.

That is how I was trained. Get in the now. Break through that denial—a very confrontational form of therapy. I was uncomfortable with it. I was uncomfortable with it because there's a part of me that does not like confrontation. And so, my personality is to allow clients to explore these at their own pace.

Let's look at the remaining elements of the script:

"There are parts of you that are helpers; parts that support you; parts that provide assistance to other parts. Sometimes they do not get the recognition they deserve, but at this moment, you can pay attention to the parts, even thinking about the parts for their supporting roles and seeing how they want to come alongside other parts and help you to be your best."

For many clients, they have never considered these parts. It's really revealing. A lot of my clients tell me they feel alone. If you work with lonely clients, help them recognize the parts of themselves that are helpers. The parts that are team players.

"The symbolic parts represent our deepest needs. They are the parts that bring us security, love, expressed values, or our deepest needs. Pay attention to these parts and how you experience them. Sometimes there are parts you are comfortable with. Other times these are the parts that we find are holding us back or even hindering us. Explore these parts of you. You might notice some of these parts are always present, or they are parts that have been overlooked."

This is a basic process in helping people to begin to pay attention to their parts. I would encourage you to do two things with this script. Use the script as your own in self-hypnosis and explore your parts. I would also encourage you to use the script with some of your clients, allowing them to explore their parts. You do not even need a script.

All you have to do is remember that there are five parts that I have discussed.

If you are doing any kind of corporate work, human resources, corporate training, or working with executives, this is a great exercise to do with team members to discover their parts that could be used to solve a problem. This is one of the processes I have used with C-suite executives, helping them discover the parts of themselves that were not necessarily being brought to the strategy sessions, etc.

CHAPTER NINE:

Weight Loss and Parts Work

My goal in any kind of therapy or hypnosis is always to help clients become the best versions of themselves they can be rather than the best me that they can be or the best of themselves I think they can be. I think it is really one of the core things that separates the exceptional therapist apart from the unexceptional hypnotist. We help people become the best them that they could be, not the best me they could be. I got that from addiction counseling. A lot of addiction counselors mistakenly believe others should get sober the way they got sober. I want people to change the way they need to change, and that might not be the same way as me. I want my *them* to be the best they can be.

My weight loss clients are 400-pound guys. I only work with men, and I only need to work with men who need to lose half their body weight. I am not interested in doing a one-off coming to me for a weight loss hypnosis session. Some of the clients I have worked with for a year and a half or two years. My typical weight loss client is a forty-eight-year-old male. They have been ruled out as candidates for bariatric surgery, or they have had bariatric surgery years ago. If they do not lose weight in the next twenty-four months, they will probably die.

That has been my niche in weight loss since around 2004. I don't do single sessions with them—my strategy is three or four sessions. I do the things I need to do to get momentum and make them successful.

Even today, I'm a firm believer with my weight loss clients that they need to see results in the first week, so my first two sessions are fairly structured. I want my clients to experience the small wins and successes. Once we are into week three, eight, twelve, or seventy-two, whichever is best for them, I can really have a chance to explore parts and how it relates to their success with losing weight or the difficulties they have had in maintaining momentum, etc.

The flip side of that is I might have a client who comes into the very first session and says, "You know, Richard, I've tried a lot of ways to lose weight. In fact, there has only been one time when I've been successful. I lost 200 pounds, and I kept it off for a few years, but then there was a part of me that decided, 'I'm going back to being the big me.' And that part I've not been able to get back." You might have a client who literally comes in for the first session and tells you their problem is parts.

The interesting thing about parts therapy is that this is a metaphor the real world uses without knowing anything about, for example, Sigmund Freud, Richard Schwartz, Gordon Emmerson, Charles Tebbetts, etc. Clients will talk about their parts. You will hear a lot of language like, "That part of me." "A part of me does this, and a part of me does that." It's a metaphor that the client may very well bring to the first session. In that case, we can use this as a strategy with them. When I teach you ideas or strategies, the idea is not to put them into every session. The idea is to add these techniques or strategies when they are appropriate for the clients who we are working with and when they would be beneficial to them.

Many hypnotists pontificate, "Why would I do six sessions? I only need to see them once while I use the XYZ process, and they're all better in five minutes. One and done." That is what some hypnotists tell us on their websites, but that is not actually what clients want.

As you work with your clients, you should be getting results, but you should also recognize that doing the shortest number of sessions is not necessarily a goal because clients want to come back. When I work with my smokers, I do three sessions with them, even though none of them need that third session. The third session is almost always high fives. It's a very easy session. But they come back for that third session. Why? Because they benefit from it, and they can grow from simply being a non-smoker to a person who is stepping into a new pattern of behavior that is resourceful for them.

Floatation therapy happens in a lightless, soundless tank filled with Epsom salt water heated to skin temperature in which you will drift into a meditative state. You get to just be with yourself and meditate or splash or whatever you want to do for sixty minutes until the timer goes off. It is an awesome experience, and people do that every week. Why? Because it feels good. It helps them. I'm a firm believer that hypnosis benefits people. I have been doing self-hypnosis for thirty-seven years, and it benefits me. I'm not a believer that I only need to do self-hypnosis once, and then I'm done.

There is a hypnotist, an ICBCH member in Seattle, Anthony Gitch. He operated a successful massage therapy business. His idea is that people go for a massage or floatation therapy because it brings them a feeling of happiness, joy, relief, growth, engagement, or whatever it is they feel. Why would we not do that with hypnosis as well?

CHAPTER TEN:

Diagnosis and Parts Work

Dissociative identity disorder is a psychiatric diagnosis. It is one that mental health professionals should be addressing. I think very few mental health professionals are actually qualified for treating this diagnosis. In fact, I think the diagnostic criteria for dissociative identity disorder are fairly useless. It requires four things, and I experience all of them on my day off! The current criteria for diagnosis really read more like a work in progress than a scientifically validated construct.

The same part dynamics work in psychiatric disorders as well.

A therapist doing therapy with somebody with a catastrophic diagnosis like dissociative identity disorder or personality disorder probably uses the same sets of skills and strategies to a large extent, and that is perfectly okay. We can see how flexible this is.

Parts therapy applies to our self-improvement and the clients who we are working with, including:

- catastrophic clients
- clients with ordinary day-to-day problems

- spiritually inclined clients who would like to find deeper meaning
- clients focused on their physical health and wellness and recovering from illness
- anybody simply trying to enhance their life

CHAPTER ELEVEN:

Ego State Therapy

It's been about twenty years since Gordon Emmerson wrote his book, *Ego State Therapy*. It has long been one of my favorite books, and it has some excellent ideas. It's not a particularly long book, but it's filled with great conceptualizations of parts therapy or what Emmerson calls ego state therapy. It's also a tremendous resource because it has practical applications. It's a book that I would recommend if you want to study the ideas of ego state therapy or parts therapy in more detail, especially if you're a clinician who is working with clients.

Emmerson developed his ideas of ego state therapy decades ago.

As we begin to look at the interventions and practical solutions we can provide to our clients, we can draw a line between the ideas and the solutions that we are able to offer them. Ego is defined by Emmerson as "the me that is inside of me." This *me* is comprised of many different parts. These are the ego states that we have. Emmerson has given a lot of thought to these ideas. You will recognize that some of the ideas correspond with the ideas of other therapists in this field.

One of the things that I think is important to recognize is that Emmerson teaches us that the ego states cannot be eliminated. Our goal in therapy is not to get rid of any ego states but rather to do what is possible, and this is to help change the ego states. One of the sections of his book is titled Ego State Therapy for Personal Development. The idea of personal development is for *me* to retain the aspects of *me* that are resourceful and beneficial and to step into a higher awareness or a higher consciousness or a peak level of performance—whether that is academic, sports performance, relationship, metaphysical, or spiritual. The idea here translates, I believe, directly into the work that we do. We're not going to be getting rid of any parts or ego states in our work. Rather we will be helping these ego states to become mature, healthy, vocal, or resourceful.

The second thing that Emmerson tells us is that ego states technically represent themselves with age. Most of the time, that age is younger than the client. For example, a client might identify an ego state they call Mr. Resourceful. If we were to ask our clients to explore the idea that Mr. Resourceful might be a younger age than their true age. For example, they might be sixty-six, and their Mr. Resourceful might be thirty-six.

Why is this, you might ask? It is often because we look at the development of these ego states from the vantage point of the age at which we became aware of them, or the age at which they matured, or the age at which they seem to operate. Even though I'm pretty healthy at age fifty-six, I was a lot stronger and perhaps in better health when I was thirty-six. This is a part of the aging process. This is one of the things that I think is important for us to recognize because our clients, especially older clients, will sometimes lament the ego state that is younger than them versus what they would consider the reality of their experience now. That incongruence can cause some pain or difficulty. But when we help our client recognize that that youthful ego state remains a youthful ego state, we can, at any age, tap into the power, strength, awareness, or wisdom of that ego state.

The third idea that Emmerson gives us is that ego states can hide. They can become inactive. Those parts of us that are repressed, hidden, or that we've pushed from the surface are the parts of us that we're uncomfortable with, the parts of us that we haven't developed, or the parts of us that we're ashamed of or embarrassed by for several different reasons. This is why these parts, these ego states, can become inactive. Ego states are a part of a person. They are not a separate person. We have an ego, and that ego has ego states, and those ego states have ego states. These are really some parts of our personality.

Ego states have an identity. Emmerson calls this the executive when that ego state is in the conscious mind—when that is the state that is present and operating. In my model, I called this the associative state. We can see some overlapping parallels between the different models, which are really just a different name for an idea that I previously explored. Emmerson observes that our ego states operate from emotions. They have feelings, and these feelings will always be present. It is a therapeutic approach that considers emotions. One of the things I discovered with my clients is the importance of helping them expand their repertoire of words that describe human emotion. It can be a great tool for helping a client understand different parts of their personality or their ego strengths or ego states or their parts.

The last big idea that Emmerson shares in the opening part of his book is the dissociation between the different ego states. The different parts that we have, depending on the person, can be more pronounced or less pronounced. In other words, we may have an easy time accessing some of these ego states because they are present. They are close to us. They are with us, and they are communicating with the other parts of us. But some of these ego states may be divorced from each other, not communicating with each other, and, to some extent, even unaware of each other. The idea here is to introduce these ego states by fostering communication. We can open up a dialogue to help us become stronger, more effective, and resilient and function at our peak performance emotionally in our relationships, in our spiritual life, and in all these other aspects.

Emmerson gives us three goals of ego state therapy. The first is to locate the different parts we have and what needs those parts have. The second element is to create communication between these different parts. Interventions based on Emmerson's ideas include a lot of dialogue, communication, or conversation between the parts. The third element or hallmark of our goal with ego state therapy is to help our ego states benefit us. This is an optimistic view of the process, an optimistic view of what our potential is. It speaks to the fact that Emmerson shares an idea with Milton Erickson: we have within us the resources to face, challenge, deal with, or do just about anything.

In the first couple of chapters of Emmerson's book, he does some speculation. He bases things on his own experiences. He shares the idea of the wisdom of other authors. One question that's often asked is, "How many ego states do we have?" Emmerson tells us that anywhere from five to fifteen different ego states are typically operating within a short period of time. But there may be an infinite number of parts or ego states within us that we can bring to the surface and into operation.

These ego states come from an idea presented by the Swiss psychologist Jean Piaget that the various developmental stages we go through are states of conflict as we grow. Emmerson claims that these ego states originate from our traumas, our conflicts, and our need to develop a part of ourselves to resolve, overcome, or deal with different situations.

Emmerson talks about underlying and surface ego states. These are either those that are associative, the ones that are present with our clients at any given time, or those that are underlying. These might be the repressed ego states that are far from immediate access yet can still serve a purpose and be resourceful when we bring them from an underlying state into a present experience.

The question might be asked, "How long will these ego states last?" Emmerson tells us that they are most likely lifelong components of our personality. We develop these early on in life, although they can emerge or develop at any point during our life through the various stages. I think this corresponds with Piaget's stages of development. The different ego states manifest and become present. They remain with us, really, throughout the rest of our lives. A question is asked of Emmerson in his book about getting rid of an ego state. We do not want to eliminate them. This is a task that would not be healthy. Rather than getting rid of an ego state, we can change or adapt to them or accept them.

To put this in context, we might get a call from our client who says, "I just had a traumatic breakup. I would like you to hypnotize me to forget my partner. I don't want to remember them." We know that this is not something that's healthy. It's not something that can be done nor something that should be done. Rather, what we can do with that person is help them deal with grief, understand loss, and recognize that they shared a part of themselves with somebody else who shared a part with them and that the sharing is no longer taking place. But they are autonomous, valuable, and resourceful. They can live fully in the present moment even though the quality of that relationship has changed and even though the relationship might not be there anymore.

At what point do we no longer develop ego states? According to Emmerson, most of our ego states are fully developed by the time we're in late adolescence or early adulthood. It's possible they could emerge at any time. In my own life, I recently went back to grad school even though I have already completed a master's degree and a doctorate and completed my Master of Business Administration in business marketing. To this point, my education and my life experiences have focused on psychotherapy, community development, and cross-cultural engagement. Lately, I've been really focusing on developing a part of me that focuses on understanding and implementing business practices. At fifty-six, I feel as if I'm creating new ego states through the learning that I had.

We can make significant changes at various points in our lives. Emmerson answers this question in his book, "Are not ego states just like dissociative identity disorder?" He calls it multiple personality disorder because, in the early 2000s, multiple personality disorder (MPD) was the diagnosis in DSM-III and then changed to dissociative identity disorder (DID) in DSM-IV.

No, Emmerson tells us, ego-states are *not* just like DID. While the methods of parts therapy might be useful to clinicians working with patients with dissociative identity disorder, the reality is that in the work that we do, this is a different type of client. Their ego states are fractionated parts of a personality that cannot communicate with each other. Ego states and multiple ego states are the normal experiences of our personality, whereas dissociative identity disorder is a specific psychiatric diagnosis. It is a manifestation of a different phenomenon, even though it may have some things that look similar on the surface.

I'm a big fan of staying within our scope of practice unless you have specific training and licensure to work with individuals with dissociative identity disorder. The reality is that those are not clients that most of us will be working with and certainly not the focus of any of the ideas in this book.

CHAPTER TWELVE:

Gestalt Therapy

In Emmerson's book on ego state therapy, he spent most of the pages talking about different hypnotic techniques and facilitating dialogue between the parts. Hence, the parts come together and have a meeting of the mind.

This correlates to the parts ideas of Richard Schwartz and internal family systems therapy. It contrasts with the ideas of transactional analysis or Sigmund Freud, which are psychoanalytic in perspective— we become aware of the parts rather than creating a dialogue or conversation between the parts.

Let's rewind to the 1940s for a moment. German-born psychiatrist Friedrich "Fritz" Perls and his wife Laura developed gestalt therapy. One of the things I love about gestalt therapy is that it's not about reliving the past or what we're going to do in the future. It's all about the experiences that can be created now.

Early in my career as a substance abuse counselor, I was trained in some of the methods of gestalt therapy with a very popular approach. This is where confrontation took place. In group therapy, a patient once sat on what we called then a "hot seat." They would be confronted with gestalt techniques. Gestalt therapy was often viewed as something that was in your face.

The reason Perls was in their face was not to be mean. It was to bring them to the present. It was to break through denial or regret or whatever else and help the person be fully present. Gestalt therapy developed the empty chair technique. It would work if the person in therapy had a chair directly across from them or next to them. In gestalt therapy, they would imagine a person or, interestingly enough, a part of them in that chair. Most often, in gestalt therapy, it would be their mother, father, spouse, or partner.

They would speak to that other person as if they were present in the chair. But Perls recognized the value of the prop because it brought the person who was looking inside of themselves to the current experience. It enabled them to really put a name and a face to that part of themselves that needed to speak to another part.

Perls recognized that we could actually put a part of ourselves in that chair and speak directly to that part. This is also what Emmerson advocates. He shares the empty chair technique or the strategy of having your client—no hypnosis necessary—have two chairs side by side or directly across from each other and have the person move from one chair over to the next chair and back to the first chair as these parts dialogue with themselves.

An example of this chair technique that comes from gestalt therapy is that we have two parts. We can have the part of us who loves to splurge and buy things like Gucci hats, Rolex watches, and first-class airfare. And then there is the part of us that wants to be financially responsible so that the money is not squandered on unnecessary items and security can be available in old age. Just take these two parts. Let's call them the secure part, which is the risk-taking part, that part that is secure and lives for the moment, and the insecure part, that part that fears preparation for the future. Our clients might label them in all different kinds of ways.

Below is an example of a dialogue between the parts. First, the therapist would instruct me, as the client, to open up communication between the parts;

"Richard, go ahead and let the secure part talk, the part that does not worry about tomorrow."

If I'm playing that role, if I'm sitting in one chair, I might say to my other part in the other chair, "Look. Eat, drink, and be merry, for tomorrow we could die. The reality is that it's nice to prepare for the future but not at the expense of enjoying the moment."

The therapist might instruct, "Okay now, Richard, switch chairs and have this part, the insecure part, speak."

I might respond as the other part, "That's all fine and dandy, but really we have advances in medical science, and we're going to live a lot longer now than previous generations did. Well, my grandfather was well prepared for his financial future. He also never anticipated living to be a hundred and five years of age. I saw how difficult that stress was for him as he got older and older and realized that money was getting lower and lower."

And the therapist might say, "How did that make you feel?"

"It made me feel sad. It made me feel scared."

"Switch roles here. Return to the other chair, the secure part. Secure part, now speak to that fear."

"I'm afraid of not being able to experience life to its fullest. I understand that financial security is important. But I would hate to look back on life and realize that I missed the opportunity to travel or the opportunity to do things I wanted to do simply because I was paralyzed by this fear."

You can see the two different parts of the personality where there is conflict can literally communicate with each other. Emmerson's empty chair technique and others that therapists have spoken of come from the concept of gestalt therapy which can be a powerful strategy or technique. As we do hypnosis with clients, I think we need to recognize that, technically, the actual hypnosis component of the session might be twenty to forty minutes. But we are probably spending an equal amount of time with them in our office during what is called pretalk, or even following a session with teaching, learning, or reinforcement of the ideas. Not necessarily being in the formal state of trance still allows us to create understanding and change and help these parts achieve their goal because, remember, Emmerson's goal with ego state therapy is:

1. To locate the parts—notice this part, notice that part.

2. To facilitate communication between these two parts because the problem, according to Emmerson, is that they are not talking to each other.

3. When they speak to each other, the goal of ego state therapy can be manifested by learning about the ego states. Both of me in these two chairs can put our arms around each other and rise to the occasion and become the best me I could possibly be.

CHAPTER THIRTEEN:

Strategies for Communicating with Our Parts

We are at the point now where we are into strategies for communicating with our parts. We can take the two-chair method and have a conversation between the parts. We can also simply direct our awareness inward as we look at the hypnotic methods of how to facilitate communication between the parts. We can have one part speak to another part.

I want to cover some core communication strategies because the amazing thing is that these strategies for effective communication with others in the world around us are actually highly effective tools for helping us communicate with our different parts.

Clinical psychologist, Arnold Lazarus gave us a model for communicating with clients as therapists. This is the first strategy. It is an acronym—SOLER. He instructed us to:

Squarely face our client

Have an **O**pen body posture

Lean forward

Make **E**ye contact with the person we're speaking with

Relax

This was his instruction to new therapists learning the skills of listening to, attending to, and communicating with clients in therapy.

This acronym has become popular in the world of therapy training and is really simple. It is an effective way to set the stage for open communication and rapport building, which is an essential strategy in any type of therapy, whether it's hypnotherapy, traditional counseling, or any other form of helpful therapy. I think there are lessons for us here as we go into the idea of communicating with those personality parts. That is, it can be a relaxing experience, although sometimes these parts have conflict, are unknown to each other, or have fear.

In the safety of a therapeutic process, relaxation and being comfortable in the moment are strategies that can open and foster dialogue. Of course, our clients will be sitting down. If we are doing hypnosis, they may even be reclining. But again, this gives us a valuable tool. This tool is to approach communication with parts unhurried and without rush. Body posture is important as it communicates to other people. They are here to attend, and we are here to listen.

Of course, leaning forward is about communicating nonverbally. We're saying, "I'm interested. I value what you have to say." In communicating with the parts, it's important that we are really open to the experiences that we and the clients have.

If we are doing the chair technique or just dialoguing with our or our clients' parts, we can decide to communicate directly to that part. I think that is really what the id has for us in parts therapy.

This is the acronym for effective therapeutic posture and positioning in communication with clients. It's something that we can teach to our clients as they begin to have a dialogue with their inner parts.

The second strategy here is a type of communication. The formula sentence I have taught thousands of clients over the years is the perfect assertive sentence. It's not passive, aggressive, or passive-aggressive. By being assertive in our communication, we increase the likelihood that our message will be heard and that it's going to be received. We will have a favorable response to it or ideally hear the response that we want. We won't always get that with assertive communication, but when we communicate assertively, we are very clear. And because we are very clear, we increase the likelihood of successful communication.

No matter what type of communication you're using in your personal life with your family, co-workers, colleagues, store people, or your clients, assertive communication goes a long way. But teaching your clients, who only know how to be passive, aggressive, or passive-aggressive, can be important. The perfect formula sentence begins with *I* because an assertive statement starts with me, not you. "*I* can only speak for myself, *I* cannot speak for you."

I feel, or I want, or I need _____.

The most important element in this entire sentence is the period. This is where we finish a feeling, a want, or a need. We are silent, and we are waiting for a response from the person with whom we are communicating.

Assertive communication is something we can use in dialogue with our parts.

Examples:

I feel as if your part of me is holding me back from accomplishing what I want.

I want some time to rise to the top and express my ideas at the moment.

I need to have a leadership role in certain situations.

I can use assertive communication with my parts. Anyone trained in Gottman therapy will recognize that the *I feel, want, need* formula sentence can actually be expressed by;

I feel _____ *about* _____, which identifies the issue. *I appreciate* _____ because gratitude is a strategy that fosters communication, and *I need* _____.

This is Gottman's communication pattern. It's really an expansion of the basic strategy of assertive communication, but again it's focused because it leads with feelings.

Going back to Emmerson's ideas, our ego states, emotions, and feelings are present with each of our ego states. We can communicate on a very emotional level with our ego states. We can tell our ego states, "I feel discounted about my role in managing money. I appreciate you trying to prepare for my financial future, but I need a Gucci hat." Again, we can use I feel . . . about, I appreciate, I need, Gottman's assertive communication as a strategy for communicating with parts either in or outside of hypnosis.

A questioning approach is an approach that Emmerson articulates. There is an idea, and this idea is small talk, getting to know somebody. The idea is "search talk," getting to know them deeper. We can and should question our parts as we learn about those parts. I could ask a part;

"When did you develop?"

"Why have you not been present more often?"

"What is it that you bring to the table?"

"How can we work alongside each other?"

"How can I support you?"

Questioning our parts is a strategy in the dialogue of parts therapy. One of the things that speakers learn is that authentic communication coupled with a connection equals engagement. If we want to communicate with our parts, we want to be authentic. This is really leading with SOLER. We want to create a connection by using assertive communication because that's the most powerful way, and it results in engagement. When we are engaged, we find and ask questions.

Again, each of these things ties together and communicates. The great thing about parts therapy is that it doesn't just help you to solve problems or raise your highest level of potential. It begins to become a model for effectively working with other people, and communities.

The last element as a key to communicating with our parts is to listen to our parts and to listen to them with empathy. Empathy does not necessarily mean agreement. Empathy does not necessarily mean "I endorse." Empathy simply means "I am attending, I am present, and I respect that part." Listening is an essential strategy in our communication with other people. That is where we get our suggestions.

But we can listen to our parts because our parts' largest frustration is that they have not been heard by the other parts. By simply taking the time in parts therapy to listen to what it is, my other personality parts have to say, "I can make dramatic changes. I can open a doorway to new possibilities, and I can then move from communication strategies into skill-building." We want to ultimately work with the parts to help them solve problems, lead us to higher levels of personal performance, and work together more effectively toward a common goal that is ultimately good for me. We can do that by applying models of effective communication to the strategies that we are going to use in parts therapy.

CHAPTER FOURTEEN:

Developmental Stages and Hypnosis Scripts

Parts work is particularly useful when doing any type of relationship work as a marriage and family therapist. I also find it useful in grief and loss counseling. I started off my career in substance abuse counseling, but simultaneously, I was really focused on grief counseling. I was the associate pastor of Servants of Christ Church. Any pastoral worker knows that grief and loss are a big part of that job. Of course, because I was working with substance users, grief and loss tended to be a frequent topic. I found that parts work was really helpful there as well. There is a video I posted on YouTube of me doing a grief session. You will see that there are a lot of parallels to some parts work. https://www.youtube.com/watch?v= EAYCpEvxKfE

My hope is that you can make it relevant by using the scripts, ideas, and concepts presented, either covertly or overtly, to benefit you or your client and to help you understand different perspectives.

Let's now focus on a little discussion of the developmental stages because developmental stages are not really a component of parts therapy. You can see where parts can emerge in conflict stages of the developmental theory.

It is interesting that Emmerson and others have written about when it is that parts become part of our personality. You can almost see a correlation to either Piaget's four stages of development or, more specifically, to Erikson. Erik Erikson really defined, I think logically, the conflicts that each of us faces in the different developmental stages of life.

Some of you are familiar with this even if you don't know who Erik Erickson was specifically, but you will recognize the seven stages of Erik Erikson's theory of psychosocial development.

Erik Erickson gives us eight stages of development and identifies the specific conflict in each.

Stage 1: Trust vs. Mistrust

This occurs from birth to around eighteen months of age. During this stage, the infant is gradually able to trust that the world is a good place and that people are generally trustworthy.

Stage 2: Autonomy vs. Shame and Doubt

This takes place from about eighteen months to three years of age. The toddler is developing a sense of independence and self-control.

Stage 3: Initiative vs. Guilt

This stage happens from about three to six years of age. The preschooler is beginning to assert their own will and desires, and conflicts often arise around issues of control.

Stage 4: Industry vs. Inferiority

At this stage, which occurs from about six to twelve years of age, the school-age child is developing a sense of competence and pride in their accomplishments.

Stage 5: Identity vs. Role Confusion

This stage is during adolescence, from about twelve to eighteen years of age. The teenager is exploring different roles and figuring out who they are and where they fit in.

Stage 6: Intimacy vs. Isolation

This sixth stage occurs during young adulthood, from about eighteen to forty years of age. The young adult is developing close relationships with others and a sense of intimacy.

Stage 7: Generativity vs. Stagnation

Taking place during middle adulthood, from about forty to sixty-five years of age, the middle-aged adult is focused on giving back to the next generation and making a contribution to society.

Stage 8: Ego Integrity vs. Despair

This last stage, Erikson believes happens, at the end of our life when we reflect back on our life and come to accept it.

It's important to realize that these conflicts, these periods of time that we go through, result in the resolution or nonresolution of those particular developmental needs. This is where parts of our personality are formed or come to the forefront. I don't think we need to debate whether or not this is where they show up or whether this is where we first become aware of them. But we have many different parts of our personalities, and to some extent, they can actually correspond with the developmental stages of somebody like Erikson.

I want to share with you something from John Bradshaw's book *Homecoming*. For those who haven't seen this book, it was very popular in the 1980s. Bradshaw was a theologian, a chemical dependency counselor, and a therapist. He had shows on PBS. He was from Houston, Texas. I was working in Houston at that time, beginning my career, so I had plenty of John Bradshaw around me to read and I became very familiar with his work. Although Carl Jung is considered the first to term "the inner child," Bradshaw was certainly one of the people who popularized the idea of the inner child.

The inner child idea is really a parts therapy idea. There's a part of us as adults that's still a child. And it's good for us to access that inner child. A healthy child ideally has wonder, curiosity, interest, and unrelenting love.

Ideally, being a kid is a pretty wonderful experience, but many people didn't get that experience—back to Erikson's developmental life stages, successful resolution of the conflict—because, through no fault of their own, their childhood was not ideal.

I grew up in Lincolnshire, Illinois. Lincolnshire. Illinois' population was 3,000 at that time. It was supposed to be perfect. It was supposed to be the ideal place. It was the quintessential America, where mom and dad raised their children. There were no problems, and life was perfect. But the reality is that life was not necessarily perfect for many people at that time, including me. Childhood was not particularly easy for me. My father was an alcoholic. He ended up dying from his addiction at age forty-two. We don't actually know if he committed suicide or whether he simply overdosed, or what exactly happened to him in the end. I was sixteen years old when he died.

When I was three, four, or five, my dad was my best friend. He was able to be my best friend because he didn't have a job. He didn't go to work because he drank beer for breakfast, lunch, and dinner. Now that I'm an adult, I realize why he was able to spend so much time with me. He could spend time with me because he was busy drinking and not busy working or doing the other things that people do.

When I was six, my mom kind of got tired of him not working and staying up all night drinking and sleeping until noon. My mom had her own issues. At age eighty-two, she still definitely manifested all the criteria of an untreated, raging anxiety disorder. I've never met anybody more anxious than my mother. That sense of insecurity was passed along to the children. When I was five, they decided to get divorced. My mom loved my dad, but he was a drunkard, so it was pretty hard to live with him.

She figured he'd go live with his mom and dad, get sober, and come back and be a responsible adult. I think that was her plan, but it didn't work out that way. Dad found another lady who liked to do drugs and drink with him. We never saw him after that. He eventually imploded because of his addiction. You can see that even though I was in the ideal place, Lincolnshire, Illinois—the perfect community—some of the families were just like my family. Things weren't working out the way they were supposed to work out.

John Bradshaw says that one of the things we need to do is go back to those developmental stages that were unresolved and allow ourselves to resolve them.

Going back to Erik Erikson: autonomy versus shame and initiative versus guilt. Purpose and will were the issues I struggled with for a long time. We can do certain things in our adult world to revisit these previous unresolved experiences and develop a new resolution. And so, this particular book is a book of exercises for each of the developmental stages. Bradshaw's developmental stages don't match up perfectly with Erik Erikson's ideals, but you can see that he probably based them on this model to a large extent.

Bradshaw goes back to the very beginning: trust versus mistrust. He writes one of the more profound meditations. Notice, however, he never uses the word hypnosis. There's a video of Bradshaw during his PBS specials, in the late eighties or early nineties, where he leads a thousand people through this meditation. It is really pretty powerful seeing the response from the audience as he guides them through the meditation.

I'll guide you through an adaption of John Bradshaw's inner infant meditation. Because some of us can look back at our story and notice that while we may have done our own therapeutic work to this point, we haven't had a chance to grieve for some of those earliest issues. We haven't had a chance to accept. Either way, acceptance doesn't mean we're endorsing or glad something happened. It simply means that we acknowledge it was present in our lives. But from a new vantage point, we can accept that the past brought us to where we are today, and then we can move on from here.

Bradshaw said, "Let's connect to the emotional part. Let's lead with the emotional part." That's really what parts therapy does, no matter whose philosophy we're talking about. One of the reasons this might have been a little controversial is that Bradshaw was not a therapist. Bradshaw was a Catholic theologian. He studied for the priesthood for many years and left before being ordained. You can see that any of his ideas are colored by a mystical, theological set of ideas. I don't mean that in the context of Catholicism specifically, but in the context of looking at the deeper meaning and a sense of connection and spirituality in his work.

This is a really powerful meditation. This is something you can adopt and use with your clients. I'm sharing it largely the way Bradshaw shared it in his book and the way he did in his lectures. I'll probably deviate a little bit from the script. There are a couple of things that I would prefer to update: times change and language changes in forty years!

According to John Bradshaw, you might want to have a Kleenex handy. When Bradshaw says this, it's actually a hypnotic suggestion, an indirect suggestion. It's an indirect suggestion that you'll get into the emotional part of the experience here.

"Go ahead and close your eyes down.

As you sit in the chair, with your arms and legs uncrossed, it is a good idea to start out by simply taking in a breath and exhaling that breath and being fully in this moment. It feels pretty good to set aside some time for yourself to learn new things, to experience processes rather than just talking about processes.

As we spend this time together over the next few minutes, we are going to take a look inside of ourselves at our previous life experiences. Become aware of your surroundings. Notice yourself in the context of time and space. Feel your back in the chair where you are sitting. Feel you are close in the body. Hear as many sounds as you can hear in the room where you are. Feel the air in the room around you. Just for now, in this moment, there is really no place you have to go and nothing you have to do. All you have to do is just be here now. If your eyes are not already closed, close your eyes down. You can become aware of your breathing, smoother and rhythmic, your heart rate calm and regular. You can feel the air as it is breathed in and breathed out. If you have any interrupting thoughts during this meditation, that is okay. You can just notice them as if they were sentences going across a TV screen during a program. Rather than following those thoughts or ideas, just recognize their presence and choose to bring your attention back to the present moment.

As you continue your breathing, you can hold on to your consciousness as much as you want, or you can let go in ways that you know will allow you to relax. You can adjust for comfort. You can swallow. You can do anything that will help you to experience this process more effectively. It feels pretty good to take this time to focus and relax, to learn, to experience when you were a child, and you learned how to hold on, and you learn how to let go, and you really know exactly how much to hold on to and how much to let go. You learned as a child the perfect balance of breathing. As an infant, you learned to breathe in and hold the breath long enough to oxygenate your blood cells. You learned to let go, to let the air out. As an infant, you learned to suck on your bottle. You learned to let go as you tasted the warm milk. You learned how to hold on to that bottle and let go when you were finished. You learned to hold on to the inside of your crib and to let go when you were ready to lie back down. You really know exactly how much to hold on to and how much to let go of.

You can trust yourself in this process to find out exactly what you need for yourself. You might notice a feeling of heaviness in your eyelids, muscles relaxing. You can feel a heaviness in your jaw and clenching the jaw. You might even notice your hands, warm and heavy; your feet, warm and heavy. Allow yourself now to experience some of your childhood memories, perhaps your first school days or your best friend in those days. You can recognize or remember a kind teacher, or a neighbor who was important to you, or the house you lived in before you even went to school. What color was the house? Was it an apartment? A house? A trailer? Did you live in the city or the country?

One of the things that is amazing about the subconscious mind is that even though we have not thought about the wallpaper in the room where we lived when we were a small child, probably in thirty, forty, fifty, or sixty years, you can probably remember the rooms inside of the house, the wallpaper on the wall, molding in the ceiling, or the doors. Wherever it was you spent your time: a special room, a special place, or a corner. Even where the dinner table was and who sat at the dinner table, and what it felt like to be at the table, and what it felt like to live in that house.

Now imagine or remember the house where your family lived when you were born. Imagine the room where you slept after you were born. See the beautiful infant that you were. Hear your voice, your own voice as you cooed, as you cried, and as you laughed. Imagine you have the ability to, in the present, hold your little cuddly self from the past. Imagine being there as a wise or gentle wizard viewing your own infancy. Who else is there? Your mom, your dad, another caregiver? Grandma, Grandpa, neighbor, sibling? What does it feel like to be born into this house with those people?

97

Now imagine that precious tiny infant is looking out at all of this, looking up at the grown-up you. See yourself as a magical person, a wizard, or even as just yourself, and feel the presence of someone who loves you. Imagine that the grown-up picked you up and held you. Hear that grown-up tenderly tells you the following affirmations. 'Welcome to the world. I have been waiting for you. I am so glad you are here. I prepared a special place for you to live.'

Our conscious mind might recognize that this was not the experience we had as a child. But it is amazing how in the present moment, we can create the experience of our adult wizard or adult self picking up this child, who we were, and affirming it by saying, 'I like you just the way you are. I will not leave you no matter what. Your needs are okay with me. I will give you the time you need to have your needs met. I am so glad that you are a boy,' or 'I am so glad that you are a girl. I want to take care of you. I am prepared to do that.'

Imagine that adult you picking up the baby and you saying, 'I like feeding you, bathing you, changing you, and spending time with you. In all the world, there has never been another just like you. God smiled when you were born.' Let yourself feel whatever you feel when you hear those affirmations. Now, let your grown-up you put the baby you down. Hear that grown-up you assure you that they will never leave you and that from now on, they'll be available to you.

Become your grown-up self again. Look at your precious little infant self. Be aware that you have just claimed that infant self. Feel the sense of that homecoming. That little infant just wanted love and will never be left alone again. Imagine walking out of the room, out of the house, looking back as you walk away, stroll forward up memory lane, walk past your first school, walk into your teenage years, walk into an early adult memory, and now, walk into the place where you are right now— feeling your toes, the energy in your legs. Feeling your chest as you take in a breath. Maybe even noticing the noise as you exhale. Feel the energy in your arms and fingers. You can even wiggle your fingers.

Stretch your arms and feel your face and be fully present, sitting in your chair, learning and experiencing, having accepted yourself."

Our experience in this process could be forgiveness. One of the things that Bradshaw also said, and I'm sure other people said it, too, was that our parents probably did the best they could with their tools. Anyone who has ever used genograms in therapy knows that families tend to repeat themselves. Approaching why is it that our developmental needs weren't met can come from, I think, a spirit of forgiveness in our adult world.

My dad was ineffective because he was a bad person. He was an ineffective dad because he was an alcoholic and drug addict. He did not have the capacity to love me as a kid because he did not have the capacity to love himself as an adult. In retrospect, I no longer have to be mad at him or hate him. Rather, I can just be the best me that I can be. I can accept that part of me that he probably drank over because it meant being responsible, caring, and engaged. It was easier to just stay drunk in the corner.

When we go back and look at where these parts of conflict emerged in exercises like this, we can move to a point of acceptance, where we see that the past brought us to where we are. Although it might have been difficult to get here, it is actually a pretty good place to be. One of the things that Bradshaw does in this book, as he goes through the developmental stages, is recognize that different parts of us emerge with different levels of resolution to the conflicts of our developmental stages.

It's okay to pick up your teenage self and hug your teenage self. It's okay to pick up your young adult self and give that young adult self an embrace and say you are okay. A lot of the ideas in Bradshaw's book really come from Thomas Harris' *I'm OK—You're OK*.

When we apply things in our own life, we can then passionately share them with other people.

When you read Bradshaw's book, you will realize that it is a little outdated. For example, he doesn't use gender-neutral language. He also had a couple of other things that are not my favorite parts of the meditation, but I ad-libbed or changed it around. It is 2022, after all!

No one ever said Bradshaw was a great parts therapist. But he was. His ideas really crossed into parts therapy. That is what I love about parts therapy. It crosses so many theoretical orientations—counseling, hypnosis, psychology, and others.

***

I created a script using the chair technique for a virtual chair technique. What I mean by that is this is really Gestalt therapy's two-chair technique or parts therapy, having one part talk to another part, but without moving the chairs. Can we do this virtually? Can this happen all inside the client's head? The answer is yes. We can do just about anything we can do in real life in our heads. Sports hypnosis can be done entirely in your head. You can play an entire basketball game in your head. You don't even have to have a ball, basket, or basketball court to have your client do sports hypnosis. We can do that in a hypnosis session as well using the chair technique.

This is a simple script that focuses on two things;

1. Assertive communication—I feel, want, or need _____.

2. The idea of the two-chair technique bringing it into a hypnosis session, where a person can just sit in one chair with their eyes closed and yet be in two chairs and speak to the other parts.

I want to share a couple of elements of the script that are important. This script needs to be adapted to the client we're working with. I left some blanks to fill in with client-specific information. So assuming that I'm working with a client, before the session, we spoke a bit about one part of them that's holding them back and another part that's doing something else for them. Maybe it's inhibiting them, maybe it's judging them, maybe it's something else. Again, we'll want to change this language based on the person we're working with. But the format is here.

"The associated part or the part that's present in the chair is your higher self, your ideal self, your present self." However the client is describing these parts.

Remember, I would prefer that my client tell me what the parts are labeled rather than me labeling the parts for the client. I'll let them know they have a creative part of the mind and to imagine another chair exactly like the chair where they're sitting, positioned directly across from them.

Notice I said, "Imagine another chair exactly like the chair where they're sitting, positioned directly across from them," rather than visualize or see another chair exactly like the chair in their position. Because everybody can imagine, but not everybody can visualize. I want to use the broadest language possible to be a more effective hypnotist.

"Imagine in this chair is another you directly across from you. You can see the other you. You can hear the other you. You can experience the other you because it is, in fact, you, another part of you within you. Of course, this is the part of you that _____."

You understand you have a pre-talking hypnosis. You are doing work with them. You know what these parts are that you're working on with them. And we can do this within the context of a complete hypnosis session.

"Take a moment to talk to that part, telling that part what you want or what you appreciate. Tell that part what you want, what you need, and what you feel. Take a moment to listen to that part of you in the other chair, to what that part shares, what this part wants, or what that part needs. Notice what you notice about communicating with the other part of you."

One of my favorite language patterns in hypnosis is "Notice what you notice." I use this a lot with my pain control clients. Notice what you notice about your experience where you reported pain. I don't want to tell them to notice numbness. Maybe they don't notice numbness. Maybe numbness is not good. I don't want to say notice the absence of pain. Maybe there's still an awareness of pain. "Just notice what you notice about these things." It's a very ambiguous request. The more ambiguous we are in hypnosis, the more profound results we find.

"Notice how these parts have been hidden and become much more manageable by speaking with the part, by listening to this part. What is your need now? Do you need to embrace this part, forgive this part, or ask for its help?"

We are asking one part of ourselves about the other part, and then imagine trading places, switching chairs in our minds.

"Notice how easy it is to switch the chairs. After all, each chair is the same you."

A little bit of confusion induction. Confusion is great in hypnosis. If it doesn't quite make sense, that's okay. The client's subconscious mind will make sense of what it needs.

"Let the part you've been speaking to lead the conversation. Let it share with you what it needs, what it wants, and how it feels. You're going to reflect back on your feelings, wants, and needs. At this point, both parts can decide. They can decide to shake hands, to hug, to sit quietly, or even to move away from each other."

Again, different clients will want a different response between the parts we're communicating. Maybe it's valuable to have distance between one part and another. Maybe it's better for one part to embrace another part.

I believe we should allow our clients to decide at the end of the process as to what it is that they would like to do with these parts. When I'm done with the session, I'll review it with my client. I'll discover with them what's going on. But this is the two-chair technique done virtually, all in the client's head—no chairs necessary.

We want to give clients time to respond between sections. For example, let me do this as if I were doing a hypnosis session. Let me do one other thing, too.

"Close your eyes now. Imagine we are doing a hypnosis session. Imagine now, in this chair is another you directly across from you. You can see the other you. You can hear the other you. You can experience the other you sitting in a chair directly across from you because it is, in fact, you, another part of you within you. Of course, that part of you is that part that really wants to learn about parts. You can greet that part. You can say hello to that part. You can even introduce yourself to that part. 'Hello, part that wants to learn. I am the part that is curious.' Take a moment to talk to that part. Start by telling that part what you want or what you appreciate about that part. You might even say to that part, 'I appreciate the effort you have put in. I appreciate and honor the care that you've made by setting aside the time for learning each week.'

Now tell that part what it is you want. Imagine, in your mind, speaking to that part, saying to that part what it is you want. You can say that out loud if you'd like to in our session right now or even in the silence of your own mind speaking directly to that part. Tell that part what you need. Take the time to do that now. Tell the part where you feel like talking to that part. Speak directly to that part, either out loud or in your own mind, telling that part what it feels like to speak to that other part. Now, take a moment to listen to that part of you that's in the chair, that part of you that's responding to each of these statements that you've made. Listen to what this part shares, what it wants, what it needs, and notice what you notice about communicating with this other part of you."

And continue with the rest of the hypnosis script.

In hypnosis, we can use dramatic pauses to give clients time to respond to the suggestions that we have made to either speak out loud or to speak in their own mind. Different clients will do different things. Most clients don't choose to speak out loud, but some do. That's absolutely fine. It won't disturb them or bring them out of hypnosis. It will actually help them to experience exactly what they need to experience in the way that they need to experience it. But the use of silence is really important.

I had a friend (Eugene Burger) who wrote a book about magic and performance in the 1980s. He had a chapter on silence as a performer. The page was blank. That's really a dramatic way of illustrating the value of silence. Sometimes, nothing needs to be said. Sometimes, we just need to give a client time in silence.

Don't worry that you're giving a client in a hypnosis session too much time. Trust me. In hypnosis, they will always use that time productively. You can even do this in a session. You can say;

"And now notice what that other part of you has to say in return. I'll give you plenty of time to listen to that part. Take the time that you need right now, with both the conscious and the unconscious mind, to listen to that part that, to this point, has not been heard."

I could give the client ten minutes if I wanted to. The client will not be unhappy.

By the way, I'm a speaker. I have always said that if the Senate ever needs to rent a filibuster, I'm the guy they should hire. I can talk nonstop. I've had to learn how to be silent. I've had to learn how to listen. It's taken practice for me to get good at it. You might not be comfortable with pauses or silence. That means you need to practice that. It's okay to be silent, to give people time. Have you ever been doing a hypnosis session, and you forgot what you were supposed to say next? Just be silent. No need to say anything. It's perfectly okay to just be silent for twenty or thirty seconds and then come back to speak. It won't disturb the client. It won't make them unhypnotized. If anything, it'll probably draw the client's curiosity closer to what it is that they're having as an internal experience. They might even find that they're irritated now that you're talking to them because their higher self is doing a better job of hypnosis than you are.

It's at this point that they may tune you out completely, no longer listening to your words and choosing their experience to process rather than engaging in the process. That's okay too.

CHAPTER FIFTEEN:

Additional Scripts

I've long been a fan of hypnosis scripting because writing hypnosis scripts is a good practice for ensuring that we're prepared when we see clients. If you're a new hypnotist, get in the habit of taking a piece of paper and writing pattern scripts that you think would be beneficial to share with clients. If you have a new client scheduled, you have some background, and you know what some of the suggestions probably could be or should be. Go ahead and type it up. You can bring that to your session if you would like to. You can use it as a guide.

I'm not a big fan of using scripts that we simply read verbatim to a client. That would not be effective. The scripts that we use should be adapted to the clients and their unique needs and concerns, as well as the presence they bring to any particular session. However, if used correctly, both by the novice hypnotist and the expert hypnotist, scripts can be a tool for assisting us in developing a deeper level of hypnotic suggestions and delivering them with confidence.

Scripting Multiple Parts

Most of us are familiar with the idea of the hypnotist who does a session, and that client is in the chair, deeply absorbed, deeply relaxed, and deeply focused on the experience. The hypnotist is doing most of the work and most of the talking. They are sharing, usually sets of suggestions that have come from our previous discussions from the pre-talk, interviews, phone conversations, and maybe even emails and intake forms that our clients have provided to us. We think of this when we often think of a classic hypnosis session.

A client who comes to you for a session probably expects that they'll sit in the chair and you'll do all the talking. I like being interactive in our sessions by having clients open their eyes, close their eyes, open their eyes, and close their eyes. I like having a dialogue with clients, asking them to repeat affirmations out loud, having them speak to their parts, and answering the questions that I have in the process.

There's no right or wrong way to do a session with clients. We might even do a session that has both components, where the client has a more passive role as I'm doing the talking and a more active role where we're having a conversation as they're experiencing deep levels of trance phenomena. These manifestations of how we would do hypnosis with a client are perfectly acceptable ideas and ways of doing that.

I meet many hypnotists who say, "I would never have a hypnosis script." The reality is that even experienced hypnotists have hypnosis scripts. They might not be written on paper, but they have done it so many times that they have committed patterns and passages and ideas to memory that they share repetitively with their clients. These are scripts as well. If we have a process, for example, the six-step reframing in neuro-linguistic programming, that's a script guiding us through those six stages of reframing with a client in a hypnosis session.

As we approach the idea of scripting multiple parts, let's recognize that there's probably not just one client sitting in our office. We're speaking to multiple parts of that client who's sitting in the chair. There may be two, three, five, or ten parts. Our client brings all their parts. When we recognize that different parts of our client's personalities are present with us, we recognize that what we need to do is to create hypnosis scripts that speak to each one of these parts that we've identified in our previous work with clients.

I want to conceptualize these three ways. The first is Sigmund Freud's idea—the id, the ego, and the superego. I'm going to share with you a script that would speak to these three parts. I'll share transactional analysis —the parent, the child, and the adult. I'll share from my model—the past me, the present me, and the future me, and how I might speak to each one of these parts.

Let's first go with the id, the ego, and the superego. I can have the client bring that part the id, that impulsive part, quickly to the action part, to the present. Let me deliver suggestions to this part. Bring the ego. The ego is that part that's ready to take action but has not tapered it with rationale yet. Bring that part as it looks at different choices that it can make. Bring the superego, that part that's judicious and makes decisions based on rational thought. Let's speak to this part. We can speak to each one of these parts in a hypnosis session. We can construct scripts that would do this.

Hypnotic Suggestion

In hypnotic suggestion, I might give a direct suggestion. An example of a direct suggestion is this: "And from this point forward, you will no longer crave a cigarette. You will notice that it seems odd to you that you no longer crave a cigarette, but you no longer will." That is a direct suggestion. I'm giving somebody a suggestion that they expect, and I expect them to act on it in response to how they feel when they're not smoking. That's a direct suggestion.

Another direct suggestion and induction might be, "And as you close your eyes down and relax the jaw, you can let the chin fall towards the chest a bit."

We're telling people what to do from start to finish in a hypnosis session. Suggestions are not just for after the induction. They will probably begin as soon as the client steps through the door. You're probably familiar with the idea of direct suggestion.

Indirect Suggestions

These could be stories, parables, metaphors, poems, songs, learnings, or different ideas that we can share with a client so that they can see themselves in the reflection of the experiences of others or in the experiences of collective wisdom. One of my favorite stories is an indirect suggestion that I have shared. It is the story of a Special Olympics event in Washington where a little boy fell and was carried across the finish line by his whole team.

Think about this in the context of parts of therapy. In my conceptualization of the parts, we have this key, the team player. Suppose I want to speak to this part using indirect suggestion, encouraging the team or parts to come to the aid of other parts. I might share these stories in indirect suggestion. I could say in a session:

"And as you continue to relax, I am reminded of a story. A story from Washington State years back that took place at the Special Olympics. All the kids were on the starting line, ready to run their race. The starter's gun went off, and they all leaped forward, hoping to be the winner. But one of the kids came right out of the gate, and he tripped and fell. He hurt his knee as he fell to the ground. He cried out in pain, realizing that everyone had passed him and that he was going to be a loser. But as he cried out, his teammates looked around one by one, seeing him lying on the ground. Each one of them stopped. Each one of them walked back. They picked him up, and they carried him together, crossing the finish line at the exact same time."

It's a great story. I've used it as an indirect suggestion of how our team parts can play a role in helping our other parts.

Process-Oriented Suggestions

We might apply process-oriented suggestions to different parts. I could use a six-parts reframe. I could use a swish pattern. I could use a demonstration of primary representational systems. I can use affirmations. I can really use any process that I'm familiar with and use in hypnosis. I can target that process to different parts of the person who's sitting in the chair in front of me. Recognize that these are all valid ways of crafting suggestions for each of the parts present in a hypnosis session.

The goal of this, ultimately, is so that our suggestions move to the post-hypnotic suggestions, the things our client is going to do after the hypnosis session that will be congruent with their preferred self or ideal self or higher self, or whatever concept of that we want to call it or that your client wants to call it. So that when our client leaves, they know that they have taken the work they have done as a to-go order. I want every one of my clients to realize that the work that we do in the hypnosis session is not something that is magic in the hypnosis session. It is magic because they created it from within themselves, and they have the ability to take it with them into their real world so that they can ultimately take action and make changes with each one of these parts that are present.

Let me share with you how we might craft some different hypnosis scripts so that you'll have a clearer idea of what you might be typing out as you rehearse delivering hypnotic suggestions using various techniques to the different parts that we have. Let's take the id, the ego, and the superego first.

Let's take an example of a person who has impulsive food choices. They say that part of their weight loss or their health journey or their motivation to come to see me was that one of the issues they wrestle with is their impulsiveness. Well, which part of us is impulsive? It's the id. The id is the immature part of us. It's the part that has to have its needs met. It's impulsive. It's quick to take action. The id might scream out, "Feed me. I'm hungry." The ego might say, "Oh, hunger is bad because that's uncomfortable." The ego might say, "Let's go to a buffet so that we can meet the need, Mr. Id, and not ever be hungry again." That's not a healthy thing to do either, though.

The superego is the part of us that comes into this: the judicial part, the moral part, the ethical part. Putting in the context of transactional analysis, maybe even the parent part comes in, moderates the situation, and says, "You go to a buffet. Make one of those healthy food choices with the correct portion."

Practicing patterns and scripts and writing these things down before your sessions will make you well-prepared when you go into the session to make sure that you share these suggestions with confidence and willpower.

The script might go like this: after an induction and deepener, I get to my suggestions for each one of these parts. I might say to my client who is in the chair:

"And to this point, you've been listening to that voice that says, 'I am hungry.' You've been hearing that voice of the id that says, 'Feed me.' You've been listening to the voice that says, 'Your needs aren't being met.' But there's another part of you. It's the ego. You may have heard it respond to the id by saying, 'Hey. Let's go to the buffet—all you can eat for $9.95. In fact, while we're there, let's prove they underpriced the sucker. And then I can eat more than $9.95 worth of food.' When you hear the voice of this part, you can actually, with your superego, call out to that voice that it's time to be silent, that the voice of reason is present. And then, while you've chosen with the superego to go to the buffet, you're going to make the decision to make one of many healthy food choices with the correct portion, even if the people you're going with choose to do something different.

For each one of these parts that are with you each and every day, you have the ability to listen or not listen. You have the ability to turn down the volume of the id and delay your hunger. You have the ability to turn down the volume of the ego that gives you unwise choices. You have the ability to amplify the learnings of the superego that helps you to make the choices that are best for you. In fact, you've come here today to make significant changes. I want to congratulate you on the choices that you've made. Because from this point forward, every time you go to a buffet, you'll see it as an opportunity to make healthy food choices with the correct portion, regardless of the choices others might choose to make."

I have a written script. I can go into a session and use this as a guide. I will probably not read it to them verbatim, but I have a guide for my session. I go into the sessions able to speak to each part, addressing each part with what is important for it to hear.

Let me give you an example from transactional analysis—the parent, the child, and the adult. My client pathologically spends money and is an impulse buyer. We're doing our session, our pre-talk, induction, and deepener; however, you want to structure a hypnosis session. "I am going to speak to the parent." "I am going to speak to the adult." "I am going to speak to the child in this situation." I might speak to them with direct suggestions or indirect suggestions, or even with processes.

Here is the way I might script a session for impulsive shopping with this type of client. I'll use an induction, deepener, and suggestive therapy techniques.

"You've shared with me that you've made choices that weren't in your best interests on multiple occasions by overspending. In fact, many of these things that you've chosen to overspend on are actually things that you already own, choosing to replace with something new rather than repair something old. You've told me that when you feel angry and you feel frustrated, when you feel a sense of urgency, your first response is to run to the mall, whip out the credit card, and buy something that makes you feel good. This part of you is probably emulating behaviors that were modeled for you.

I've discovered that most of us only do what we know how to do, and we only know how to do what we've learned to do. Chances are that your parents weren't good with money either and didn't model financial success for you. There's a parent within you that's ready to meet your needs at any moment by making choices that aren't necessarily the best choices in your best interests. The good news is that you can retrain that parent. You retrain that parent to make choices that are good for all of you.

Because there's an adult component of you that recognizes that by replicating the patterns of the family, you're creating results that are identical to what you've already seen. This adult part of you knows that by creating financial responsibility, by avoiding the interest payments of credit cards, and even saving some money, learning about the joys of compounding interest, you create new experiences in life.

There is also a child part of us. This is the part that wants what it wants. It says, 'The new person in this case will make me happy.' But it's the adult who says to the parent, 'Rather than making the child happy by simply buying it what it wants, let's make the choice. That diamond from the local cobbler, and the leather repair shop to have one of the old purses repaired.' Be able to enjoy both something new and something affordable. Noticing now how good it feels in this moment to create that awareness."

You can speak directly to each one of these parts in a hypnosis script that we craft. Here's a script for the past, the present, and the future. Let's use fear of flying as our example. I'm going to speak to the past me, the present me, and the future me in this session, or a past client, present client, and the future client in this session.

I begin with an induction, deepener, and whatever else I might do in the hypnosis session. Then I'm going to speak directly to these parts.

"There is a previous you before you came to these hypnosis sessions that was afraid to fly."

113

Notice I'm speaking to it in the past tense.

"Bring that past you to the present you that used to be afraid to fly and notice that by just bringing that to the forefront, the associated awareness of this present moment, you might even feel a little bit of anxiety or agitation because that old you was filled with fear. Let me assure the old you that the old manner of living is no longer required. You can even thank the old you for giving a warning signal and keeping you safe. You can also let the old you know that its help is no longer needed.

Because there's a new you, a new you who's not afraid to fly, a new you who's embraced the techniques of dealing with anxiety that I've shared with you. You can even tell that new you, 'Welcome aboard.' Notice that as soon as you pay attention to this part of you, the new you or the future you, you experience a sense of calm. Your breathing becomes smooth and rhythmic. Your heart rate is calm and real. This future you is filled with wonder, filled with opportunity. It knows that it can build relationships with people around the world, with family and friends, and even new business and new places. It's exciting for the new you to be present here in this chair. Notice something. The future you that steps on a plane with confidence is not something you have to hope to become. It's actually present with us here right now. Sense within you that part of you that's fully present and ready to sit on a plane.

Know that when you get ready to buy a ticket later this week, you can do it with confidence. When you get to the airport and your boarding number is called, and you board the plane, you can board with a sense of wonder. When you sit in your chair, you can sit with a sense of calmness, just as you are doing right now. In fact, the good news here is this. The good news is that you've created a sense of calm and a sense of security, and a sense of safety right here in this hypnosis session. At any time, in any place in the future that you need to be brought back to this experience that you've created here, you can do that easily."

I can even give them an anchoring tool. I can say this:

"Go ahead and touch your thumb and index finger together. Go ahead, touch them together, and press them together. As you press them together, just notice the sense of calm that you're experiencing right now. Relax your fingers. Push them together once again, and when you push them together, notice that you're aware of that sense of calm. Anytime, anyplace in the next week or two or three, in the next year, or two or three, that you need to bring yourself back to where you are right now, you just touch those fingers together. Take a breath and sense an experience of calm, knowing that it's safer to fly than drive. It's easier to fly than to walk. The world of wonder brought about by the opportunity to fly is going to open doors for you that you've never expected in life."

I've created a script based on speaking to the past, the present, and the future client, speaking to each part in a hypnosis session. By crafting scripts, we make sure that we cover each of the parts, especially when we have a complex client. Let's say you're trying to deal with the physical part, the associated part, the repressed part, the team part, and the symbolic part. We can do that and make sure we cover everything when we have rehearsed this by practicing patterns and suggestions, no matter what type of suggestions they are when a client steps from our office into the world of wonder that hypnosis allows them to create.

CHAPTER SIXTEEN:

Emmerson's Steps for Accessing Ego States

I n his book, *Ego State Therapy*, Emmerson gives us the idea of what is called a dichotomous technique for accessing ego states. If we would like to have a conversation with the different parts, Emmerson gives us a model or a set of steps for eliciting each of these parts.

We can have a more interactive session. We want to be able to speak back and forth to an individual, really having conversational hypnosis without doing formal hypnosis, or even during the formal hypnosis process where we reorient the client. We'll be able to have a conversation with the various parts.

Again, any conceptualization is correct. There is not really a right or wrong way to do hypnosis. Ultimately it is about meeting our client's needs.

The nice thing about Emmerson is that he's very polite, thanking these parts and asking permission to talk to other parts. After we have elicited all the relevant parts (not all the parts within a personality; otherwise we would be there all day), we can then go back and forth between the parts having communicated with them.

Let's look at the four steps he gives us;

Step 1.

Identify two or more parts relevant to the presenting problem. We will probably be doing this in the pre-talk or the assessment process that occurs before our hypnosis session. This could be information we gathered on the telephone. It could even be asking, "What are the parts of your personality that you are struggling with in this situation?"

It's also important to note that the clients will tell us that different parts of their personalities are struggling. They might say, "In this situation, it's as if one part of me is doing this and another part of me is doing that. One part of me wants this, and other parts of me want that. One part of me feels this; another part of me feels that." Once we identify the different parts that we are going to be speaking to during a hypnosis session, we can then go on with the rest of the process. The second part is to give a client a tutorial on the different parts and educate them to share what parts therapy is all about.

We do not have to give them all the details. I might say to a client, "You have alluded to two different parts; a part of you that wants this and a part of you that wants that. I wonder if there are other parts of you that might even be in conflict with those parts. Maybe you want to identify some more parts." I can then say to my client, "There is an approach to helping people solve problems called parts therapy. That comes from the idea that within our personalities are different parts of us. During the session, I'm going to speak to each one of these parts. I'm going to talk to each one of these parts. You're going to be able to bring each one of the parts to the present as we engage in a conversation and as I provide some hypnotic suggestions for each part. So that when you leave here today, you will be able to act in a way that is unified, in a way that is best for all of you." That is really the only explanation I probably need to give.

Step 2.

The next step is through the hypnosis session, asking the client to speak to the part that has been identified. "The part that wants this, can I speak to that part?" The client will say, "Yes." I can now speak to that part. "Tell me about yourself. What is your role?" I can ask questions. "When did you become an important part?" I can ask, "How is it that you carry out your job of doing that?"

Step 3.

I can speak to the part, and I can notice the ego state switching back and forth. When you are doing this for the client, you can see changes. You see different postures, different effects, even the flattening of the muscles in the body, a slower heart rate, a quicker heart rate, a faster pace of speech, or a slower pace of speech. As we begin to notice these switches between the parts, we know that we are communicating with the different parts of the person's personality.

Step 4.

Speak to the part, asking, "What would you like me to call you?" Ask them for permission to speak to the other parts. "Do you mind now if I take a couple of minutes to speak to some of the other parts of the personality?" They will give permission. Thank the part politely. "Thanks for taking the time with me." Then I will speak to the next part. As I speak to the next part, I will do the exact same thing. Ask what to call it and thank the part. I will then ask to speak to the next part that we identified previously.

After speaking to all the different states in order, I can then go back and forth. I can speak to each part, giving suggestions by guiding a part through a specific process or experience. This method of communicating and accessing the various ego states is a great guide for creating more interactive hypnosis sessions that help our clients meet their deepest needs with the ideas of parts therapy.

118

CHAPTER SEVENTEEN:

The Path Script

At this point, we have been focusing primarily on ideas, such as how the parts will communicate with each other, how the goal is to create a unified self, and how all the parts will work together in perfect harmony. Richard C. Schwartz wrote *No Bad Parts* about restoring trauma and creating healing in the context of Internal Family Systems theory. He gives us an exercise called The Path. It's a visualization or meditation exercise.

I'll go through it using a different script than is in Schwartz's book. The reason why I have Schwartz's script memorized is that the process is pretty simple. The idea here is slightly different from all these parts working together. In IFS, the central part is the self, the ideal self, the mature self, the helpful part, and the resourceful part. This healthy self may be surrounded by many other parts, which have been less than resourceful over time. That is one of the things as we find the part of us that can take away from our true self or our authentic self or our most productive self.

The path exercise is unlike anything I've written about so far. It's really about shedding the parts. It begins by imagining that you're going to take a journey, that you're going to be walking on a path. Again, you could change the script to be anything. You could be walking up a mountain. You could be taking a boat out to sea. What's important here is not the visualization used but the process.

It begins by asking;

"'Would you like to take a journey?' To identify the parts present at the beginning of the journey, you're going to ask your parts, 'Who is willing to stay behind? Who is willing to simply wait for the self to go on the journey?' You will discover that many parts are more than happy to simply wait and give the self the time that it needs to go on this journey and return. The self can assure these parts that, 'I will be on a short journey. I will be returning shortly.'"

Then the visualization begins, not even a visualization as much as the experience of going on this journey. Schwartz points out that anytime during this process, it becomes like a movie, where you're watching yourself, it means you've taken parts with you that didn't stay behind. These parts can be asked, "Hey, would you mind returning back to home base? Would you mind going back and waiting while I continue on this journey?"

This can be a lengthy exercise or a short exercise. The idea is to shed as many parts as possible, leaving the authentic, the beautiful, the perfect self in place. This gives the person experiencing this meditation or hypnosis session an opportunity to separate this part from all the other parts, which can then return at the end of the exercise. Below is a script for this:

"Begin this exercise by simply being open and willing to learn and experience new things. Imagine that you are going to be going on a journey. In this case, let's call it a walk. Go ahead and close your eyes down if your eyes aren't closed down yet. Imagine the beginning of this walk, where you are present—the self with your parts. The pieces of your personality that have both been a resource to you, as well as those parts of the personality which have perhaps been less than resourceful to you. Address these parts. There may be three, four, seven, or eight of these parts, maybe even more. Address these parts in your own mind and let these other parts of your personality know that the self is going to be taking a short journey. Say to these parts, 'Parts, I'm going to be taking a short journey. I'd appreciate it if you would simply wait here while I go on this journey. I'll return.' See which parts are willing to remain behind at what we'll call home base.

When all the parts have decided to remain behind, begin the journey. Begin the walk, taking the first few steps away from the other parts, stepping a few more steps, looking back, and noticing if any of these parts are following you. As these parts follow you, it's okay to take the part with you on some of this journey. But you can also ask that part, 'Would you be willing to return for a little bit as I continue this journey?' Let that part go back.

As you imagine your steps, as you imagine walking, it could be through the woods or through an open field, it could be on a path or even along the water, simply pay attention to the part of you that we call the self. The part that is functioning. The part that is resourceful to you. The part that is meaningful to you. The part that is the best to you. Continue on this journey in your mind's eye. Notice something; if you become an outside observer of the scene, watching it like it's a movie, you've probably continued to bring some of those parts with you. You can simply ask those parts, 'Parts, would you mind going back and waiting?' Shut yourself off from those parts, continuing to walk, leaving only the ideal self, the self that is the true you. Continue on this journey, noticing the feelings, the emotions, the awareness of the truly beautiful, unique self that is you.

Of course, if you notice any parts are still following or are still present with you, you can ask them to return. Let them know. Say, 'I'll be back shortly.' If they won't go, it's okay to actually return back with them and to continue this journey on another day. But if they've gone back, leaving that true, fit, beautiful, pure you, continue that journey, noticing where it leads and what it feels like to be in this time and in this place, and in this space. Take as much time as you need with yourself to see yourself as you truly are, to see yourself with the resources needed in any situation. To respond in a way that is good to you. To respond in a way that benefits you. To be present in a way that solves any obstacle in your way with a new perception of the self, noticing your strengths, noticing your resources.

When you're ready, you can simply turn around. You can walk back quickly or slowly to the other parts, returning back to home base, letting the other parts see you as you truly are. Develop a new relationship with the new you that you have discovered on this journey. Go ahead and take in a breath. Pay attention to the chair where you sit, the air in the room around you. If your eyes aren't open yet, go ahead and open the eyes. Stretch out any muscles that need to be stretched. Notice the smile on your face and how you feel. Your heart rate is smooth and rhythmic. Your breath is calm and regular. Having completed an exercise called the path, the path leading, of course, to a relationship with the true self."

CHAPTER EIGHTEEN:

Carl Jung Self-Realization, Shadow self, and Archetypes

To truly understand the depth of the potential work we can do using parts therapy, we have to go back in time back to Sigmund Freud's time. His contemporary Carl Jung came up with a series of ideas that have been as influential as Freud's work in understanding personality, parts work, and ways of creating interventions to help people.

Even though it's been more than a century since Carl Jung postulated his ideas, they're still at work. Many of the modern approaches to therapy used today have an underlying understanding of Jung's ideas and the methods he offered us. It's interesting to note that the current research into the effectiveness of Jungian therapy shows that those who engage in a path of using Jungian therapy in order to experience or make changes are individuals who are likely to reduce future medical costs in psychiatric settings, likely to reduce relapse in clients, or likely to rise to a higher level of performance.

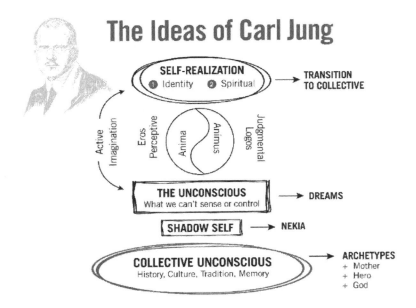

The Ideas of Carl Jung

SELF-REALIZATION
❶ Identity ❷ Spiritual → **TRANSITION TO COLLECTIVE**

Active Imagination
Eros Perceptive
Anima
Animus
Judgmental Logos

THE UNCONSCIOUS
What we can't sense or control → **DREAMS**

SHADOW SELF → **NEKIA**

COLLECTIVE UNCONSCIOUS
History, Culture, Tradition, Memory

→ **ARCHETYPES**
+ Mother
+ Hero
+ God

The graphic above is a good visualization of the depth of Jung's ideas. Jung was a psychiatrist and a mystic. He bridged that gap between mental health and metaphysical health. His work was colored with spiritual and religious ideas, and ideas that went to the core of our understanding and our connection to human beingness, which is a set of profound ideas.

As we have discussed parts therapy, I've shared many different theories, conceptualizations, and ideas. In Jung's work, the idea of parts, even though he never expressed it as parts therapy, is definitely a foundation for much of what we understand today in modern parts work.

Diving into the major components of Jung's model and his ideas, let's look at that part of self-realization. The goal of being in therapy is to move to a point where we have self-actualization and self-realization. We know who we are. We are comfortable with who we are. We are accepting of who we are. We utilize our internal strengths and resources. All of these embody the concept of self-realization. Self-realization is having a firm identity and knowing how to use that identity to navigate the different scenarios or situations a person experiences.

Jung said that identity emerges in the first part of life. This is childhood, adolescence, and young adulthood. Self-identity emerges as a person focuses inward and on themselves. But in middle age, a person's path becomes more spiritual. They look for a sense of connection to other people. Carl Jung called this a "transition to the collective" that's made in the latter part of life. This is the time when people are more tempered, more engaged, and seek to leave a legacy. Jung put all elements of this second part of self-realization in the context of life stages—early life and later life stages.

As a central idea, Jung has something that I created on the graphic as the Dao. The Dao is an ancient Chinese idea that everything has two parts. You may be familiar with the yin-yang symbol. For Jung, there were two parts central to our self-realization. These were the anima and the animus. The anima is the feminine part of us. Jung believed that everybody has a feminine part, both males and females. The animus is the masculine side of our identity and our spiritual self. Every one of us has an anima and an animus.

The predominant idea in Jung's work was a division of the parts of self-realization into masculine and feminine parts or components. Jung described this feminine side as the perceptive side, the erotic or the eros side, and the masculine side as the judgmental side, the logos, and the rational side of our thinking.

Below is the unconscious mind in Jung's concept. Jung stressed working in the unconscious, and many of the methods of Jungian therapy are based on working in the unconscious mind. According to Jung, the unconscious mind is the part of our mind that we cannot sense, that part of the mind that we cannot control—its core, breathing, respiration, survival. But it's that part of us that is hidden from us. It's that part that we do not know. He labeled this part of the unconscious mind as the shadow self.

The shadow self is an essential concept in Jungian therapy. Jung believed that for us to achieve self-realization, we needed to bring this shadow part out into the open. Jung used an approach called Nekyia. This is an ancient practice of conjuring up the spirits of ghosts and asking them about the future, which is a really interesting idea in the context of our own shadow personalities or ghosts.

The movie *Fight Club* is probably the best example of this from popular culture is. In the movie and book, there's a narrator. This is the character who works in an office and does everything he's supposed to do. He's introduced to a character named Tyler Durden. Tyler Durden is rough and tough, and he fights and does drugs. The narrator is intrigued by Tyler Durden and the life he lives in, which is entirely different than his. Of course, the narrator becomes a colleague, a friend, and a person who works with Tyler Durden. The book and the movie reveal that Tyler Durden is actually the narrator's shadow self. Tyler Durden shoots and kills the narrator in the movie's final scene. But the narrator is then free. The narrator is free to become himself now that he's explored the dark side. Of course, the movie *Dr. Jekyll and Mr. Hyde* is also about the idea of the shadow self.

I want you to think now about your own personality. What is that part of who you are that nobody knows? Each one of us has a hidden part, a hidden part of our unconscious mind, with drives and desires and ambitions of its own that we have, perhaps, hampered because it is the right thing to do. But we have that within us. This is our shadow personality. This shadow wants to come into the light in order for us to achieve self-realization. Jungian therapy is fascinating because it's willing to explore what many characterize as negative or uncomfortable ideas and thoughts.

Earlier, I gave you my conceptualization of parts therapy, using the acronym PARTS—the Physical, the Associated, the Repressed, the

Team, and the Symbolic self. As we wrestle with the idea of our symbolic self, I believe part of that is the Jungian component of our shadow self. This is one of its parts. As I continue discussing ideas related to Jung, you can put it in that box or set of tools for understanding the symbolic self.

How does Jung go about helping people? What does the therapeutic approach entail? An active imagination is one of the key concepts in Jungian therapy. He used active imagination as the bridge between the unconscious and self-realization. Jungian therapy is filled with ideas, methods, and techniques that draw on active imagination, helping a person experience and see things differently than they have ever experienced, seen, and understood before. Jung's techniques and strategies deal with dreams.

There's a big difference between dream analysis that says, "Well, if you dream about green, that means money" or "If you dream about flying, that must mean you're anxious" and dream analysis that does not try to attach a specific meaning from an external source and seeks rather to connect the inner meaning with the dream. This will make each analysis different and unique. For one client, green might mean money; but for another client, it might mean deep water.

Perhaps the client keeps a dream journal, and they talk about their dreams as we help them recognize that dreams are fragments of the conscious experience in the unconscious mind. Dreams often make no sense to us with the conscious mind. They often have no order. They seem to be just coming out of nowhere. But the reality is, according to Jung, these dreams are seeded in the unconscious mind and in our shadow self. By becoming aware of our dreams and looking at the parts in the context of active imagination, we can move to the point of self-realization.

All of these are predicated on a very interesting idea of Jung's. This is the idea that a part of us is the collective unconsciousness. The collective unconsciousness is different from my unconsciousness. My unconsciousness is about me. The collective unconsciousness is really our history. It's our culture, our memory, our tradition, and our narratives. It's all these things that connect us to everybody else who is currently in our world and those who have preceded us. This goes back to Jung being a mystic and his ideas of Nekyia and asking the ghosts of the past to tell us the future.

Jung believed we were born with collective unconsciousness. This is our connection to both the past and the present. This is the part of ourselves that's not independent. This is the part of us that draws on all those collective experiences that we have had as a culture, society, and human race. Of course, many other people have brought this idea that sounds crazy into their work. The idea is that in trauma, the body keeps the score, then it's stored within us. It's an idea that parallels the collective unconsciousness and that we can carry the traumas of our previous generations into our present experiences. For the hypnotist, dealing with the concept of the collective unconsciousness brings about all kinds of possibilities in therapy.

Jung is also known for developing the idea of archetypes. These are the universal representations that we have about certain things from our collective unconsciousness. For example, we all have a concept of what a mother is, what a hero is, and what God is. These archetypes come from our collective unconsciousness. Carol Pearson and Margaret Mark took the work of Jung and his idea of archetypes and divided it into twelve archetypes. This was, to some extent, to compete with the Myers-Briggs type indicator to produce a different understanding of the personality. I think it's important to recognize that there are an infinite number of archetypes that Jung believed were possible and that we can tap into. To some extent, while these archetypes are outside of us, they come from our collective unconsciousness. Those beliefs and emotions become a part of us.

Through therapeutic processes, both in and out of hypnosis, we can move our clients to a point where they have transitioned to a collective contribution as a result of meeting their shadow self (this part of them is hidden from others and sometimes even hidden from themselves) by learning about their unconscious self and their parts—back to my model PARTS—the repressed parts, which are buried deep in the unconscious mind, both from a personality perspective, and maybe even from an experiential perspective, or from a traumatic perspective, etc. reside here. This idea of becoming familiar with the anima (the feminine side) and the animus (the masculine side) is really an interesting idea.

I have created a drawing of Jung's idea, which expresses almost every idea that this influential therapy has related to parts therapy.

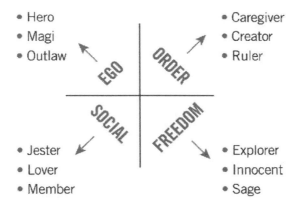

JUNGIAN ARCHETYPES
(Margaret Mark & Carol Pearson)

CHAPTER NINETEEN:

Smoking Cessation and Habit Control

Scripting can be done for multiple parts because if we have a client who is coming in, no matter what the problem is, there are going to be multiple parts that are contributing to resistance to change. These multiple parts are going to embrace unhealthy behavior as the solution. There will be parts that meet their needs.

Every dysfunctional behavior meets needs. Ronald David Laing, a psychiatrist, had the belief that all madness has meaning. I really believe that's true. No matter what our client is doing, they're doing it not because they want a screwed-up life.

Nobody ever called me up and said, "Hey, Richard, I'd like to make a therapy appointment. I'm forty-three years old. I'm three times divorced. I live in a van down by the river. I keep warm by burning trash in a fifty-five-gallon drum. I drink MD 20/20 out of a plastic bag. I'd just like to come in and process having achieved all my life goals." When they come to me, they typically say, "I'm doing . . . , and it's causing me a problem."

And yet they continue to do it. And they do it because even those unhealthy behaviors meet the legitimate needs of the clients. So let's explore that idea for a moment. Let's say I'm a cigarette smoker. Elman did the famous 1, 2, 3 cigarette smoke induction. A smoker smoking cigarettes knows it will kill them and give them cancer. It says that on the side of the pack of cigarettes. Why is it that smokers smoke? It changes your emotion. It might not make you feel better. It might even make you feel worse, but at least you don't stay the same. That's actually really an important reason why people smoke.

Another reason is that smokers have a five-minute break. The rest of their colleagues are in their cubicles or workplaces having to work through the whole hour. But smokers have figured out how to take a break. They are doing deep breathing exercises. So these are the reasons why people smoke. I mean, there are a hundred reasons why people smoke because in the moment, it always does something positive for a person. When your client comes to you with negative behaviors, actions, and self-defeating behaviors, it's because those behaviors meet legitimate needs. And those legitimate needs are the legitimate needs of different parts of them.

You can conceptualize that there's a part of them that needs a five-minute break and needs to be away from other people and take a time out. There's a part of them that smokes a cigarette because it gives them energy, the physical part of them that needs energy. That's why the average cigarette smoker smokes two or three cigarettes to get going in the morning, even before they have a cup of coffee. There's a part of them that's uncomfortable with their emotions.

Each one of these legitimate needs is a legitimate need of a part. And in parts therapy, we can take an unhealthy behavior, look at the legitimate needs, and discover what the parts are based on the needs being met through each of these behaviors.

Let's take a look at another popular subject in hypnosis—weight loss. What legitimate needs are met through the behaviors that obese clients engage in? What baby behaviors do they engage in? They engage in being a couch potato. What does that do for a person? What needs are met by being a couch potato? You don't have to think. You just exist.

You push the world away. And the world's not coming to you. And if you aren't going to engage in it, you can keep your distance from the world. You may also feel like you don't have to be responsible for things going on.

A need is met by letting somebody else take control of responsibility. "A part of me wants somebody else to do it for me."

Another reason may be the rebellious child inside would make their parents crazy if they were a couch potato. So they'd love seeing their parents losing their minds over them being on the couch all day long. You can get even with somebody. You can be passive-aggressive in your behavior. All of these are different parts. "There's a part of me that wants you to take control. There's a part of me that wants to be passive-aggressive. There's a part of me that wants to avoid physical pain. If I'm a couch potato and I go for a walk today, I'm going to be sore tomorrow even though that was a very moderate activity or exercise. So, there is a part of me that wants to avoid physical pain."

As a couch potato, there is self-soothing or self-care going on, maybe as Freud said about infantile oral fixation. There is that infant within us who demands to be self-soothed and have a longer nap.

Let's take the behavior of an obese person who knows what healthy food is and still eats fried chicken, tacos, and churros and tops it off with peach cobbler and apple pie. They know that's not healthy. Why do they continue to make unhealthy food choices? What does it do for them?

It's easier not to be responsible for yourself. Somebody else will be responsible for you. In this case, the healthcare system.

Some of these foods are addictive, too, given the sugar content. Along with addiction to food from a physical perspective, there's also the psychological obsession. This is a person's craving for high carb, low nutrient foods. Why? Because it provides instant energy, even though that energy doesn't last in the long run. Other needs are met through eating unhealthy foods; for example, a chicken fried steak makes you feel good and is soothing.

We can create an association with our food that might be associated with something pleasurable, even if the food is unhealthy. For example, my great-grandmother took a job at a Swedish bakery so she could learn how to bake delicious food. Our family tradition is Swedish pizza, a Swedish butter cookie covered with lingonberries and then frosting on top of it. It is pretty darn awesome. And when I eat that, it makes me think of my great grandmother, Momo, who was awesome.

The other thing about unhealthy food is that it's more convenient to eat unhealthy prepackaged food. You can just go buy food at the drive-thru window and chow down. It is much more convenient than doing dishes or waiting for food to be prepared.

Legitimate needs are met through every one of these unhealthy behaviors. And every legitimate need that's met is really a part of us.

So when we are scripting for parts, we have to ask: What is the behavior? What legitimate needs are being met by the behavior? Then we can craft suggestions, either indirect or direct suggestions, or process suggestions to each of these parts that retrain them, repair them, and reframe them. Those are some of the ideas for scripting that I think are important and useful. Now let's take a look at the graphic for the dichotomous technique. This is again based on Emerson's book.

Dichotomous Technique for Accessing Ego-States

(GORDON EMMERSON, PH.D., 2002)

1. Identify two or more parts in your pre-talk
2. Give clients a "tutorial" on parts work
3. Hypnotize client, asking to speak to the first part
4. Notice the state switches between parts through the process
5. After speaking to the part ask what to call it, and gain permission to speak to other parts.
6. Thank-the state
7. Speak to each state. Returning to gain permission and thank the part.
8. After speaking to all parts present, switch it up based on utility and speak back and forth until all goals are accomplished.

Let's identify two or more parts and the examples we have given here for the smoker or the non-smoker. Our clients don't know that each one of these legitimate needs is an expression of a part of them and that we're made of many parts. In our hypnosis session, I'm going to give suggestions to these parts such as:

"There is a part of you that knows smoking is unhealthy, but there is a part of you that wants to get away from other people. There is a part of you that knows not exercising and eating unhealthy food is not good for you.

But there is a part of you that craves familiarity or is comforted by familiarity. There is a part of you that does not want any pain. There is a part of you that does not want the short-term pain for the long-term benefits of increasing your physical activity."

Then we'll hypnotize the client. We'll speak to the first part. This is what I like about Emerson's idea. Emerson is telling us that we can speak to one part at a time. Emerson talks about a conversational hypnosis experience.

Many hypnotists are not really comfortable with asking real questions and getting real answers. Even if the client opens their eyes, that's something to practice. If you're not doing that, ask the clients to open their eyes and speak to them for a little bit, and have them close their eyes again. That won't disturb the session at all. It will actually create fractionation and increase the hypnotic response.

But Emerson says, "Let's speak to one part, the first part." And he tells us then to notice that as the client changes, their parts will notice when the state switches when they move to a different part. We'll notice that in their effect, speech rate, posture, and muscles. We'll notice it in the tiny micro muscles of their face. A person who is in a state of deep relaxation, for example, may become waxy, almost looking as if they're like a mannequin. If you focus on the skin in a deep trance, it might be flushed and rosier as they change states.

We have physical, emotional, and linguistic cues that have changed. And then, after speaking to the part, ask,

"What do you call this part of you that has to have . . . ? What do you call this part?"

Or

"What do you call this part that says, 'I need three cigarettes before I even have my cup of coffee because I got to get going?'"

Then ask that part for permission to speak to the other parts. This is about respect, and we thank the state. For example, if the person is addicted to Cheetos:

"Thank you, Cheetos eater, for the time. I am now going to speak to that part that is intellectual, that part that knows what the healthy choices are."

I'm going to speak to this part, maybe give suggestions to this part, find out information from this part. Again, I'm going to ask permission, thank the part, and then speak to all the parts. We can have a conversation and talk back and forth with them. And that is another way of working with parts where we do that conversationally.

In Chapter 15 you have example scripts: an ego and superego are speaking to the multiple parts for eating, a script for the parent, child, and adult for a person making impulsive purchases, and a script for past, present, and future parts for fear of flying.

Take time to rehearse either speaking to the parent, the adult child in the ego or the superego, or the past, present, and future self. Practice speaking to the multiple parts to clarify the past, present, and future scenarios.

Let's consider a client coming in for anxiety and to control anger. For the client, the past me was that part of me to learn how to manage anger. And every time Grandpa was angry, he drank a twelve-pack of beer and threw a chair through the window. And every time Daddy was angry, he drank a twelve-pack of beer and threw a chair through the window. Guess what I do every time I am angry? Every time I'm angry, I drink a twelve-pack of beer and throw a chair through the window.

The past me only knows what it knows. This is why we can be forgiving of the past me. Because the past me actually did the best it could with the tools that it had. But the past me is not the future me. The future me is that person who is not going to be on probation anymore. Future me will be that person who is sober, gets out of bed in the morning, and goes to work each day. And the present me is actually me in the chair right here who has the ability to make a decision and a choice to take an alternative action, to learn something new.

A part of us is the past us, often holding us back. It's like the past me is actually holding me by the foot, keeping me from moving forward. The future me in hypnosis is our timeline therapy. That is what we know we are going to be a month from now.

136

When my smokers come in, I tell them, for example:

"And right now, of course, you are a non-smoker because you are not smoking a cigarette in this office, but I know that a month from now, a year from now, a decade from now, you will still be a non-smoker. And the reason is, I'm speaking to the future self, because the present you has made a decision. The present you has had your last cigarette. So the real question is not, how do I quit smoking for the present me? The question is, how do I stay stopped?"

CHAPTER TWENTY:

Archetypes in Depth

In this chapter, I continue discussing Carl Jung and the concept of archetypes which is a very important theme throughout Jung's approach to psychotherapy and certainly very important to us in understanding parts work as well.

We see archetypes often as a part of ourselves that represents a certain person. These can be a part of us also. But the archetypes, these parts of us, could also be our motives, understandings, learnings, and themes in life. They can also be an archetype of events in life.

Jung gives us some depth when we look at parts therapy by exploring the idea of archetypes both in events as persona figures and as motifs.

What is an archetype? An archetype is a well-known representation. It's easily understood and might come from being the first at something. An example is Abraham, the archetype of the father of faith. We have three major Abrahamic religions: Judaism, Islam, and Christianity.

And in every movie, we have a hero. That's what the movie is about.

For Jung, these archetypes were really nothing more than a conscious representation of something.

JUNG ARCHETYPAL EVENTS

+ Birth
+ Death
+ Separation from parents

+ Initiation
+ Marriage
+ Union of opposites

Conscious Representaitions

ARCHETYPAL FIGURES

Mother — Father — Child — Devil — God
Wise old man — Wise old woman — Trickster — Hero

ARCHETYPAL MOTIFS

Deluge — Creation — Apocalypse

As we provide therapy to individuals, the archetypes that they experience, the archetypes that they relate to, and the archetypes that the client is able to identify are going to be archetypes of conscious representations of their internal experiences or their knowledge.

Let's take a look at how Jung divided this. It's important to note that Jung was not rigid. There are actually an unlimited number of archetypes, but these are what are identified by Jung in his work.

The archetypal events that people can identify in their experiences when we are interviewing them or talking to them will probably refer to various archetypal events either with this language, these words, or with some other words that probably mirror these experiences. They include birth, death, separation from parents, initiation, marriage, and the union of opposites.

Birth

We know that birth is a significant event. It becomes a metaphor throughout our lifespan as we graduate from college and have a new birth with new opportunities. We survive a traumatic experience and feel like we have a second lease on life. Let's say we reset the description of the birth archetype. The religious experience of being born again is an archetype of birth.

Death

Long before our own death, we have death archetypes and experiences in our lives. We have grief when we have loss, separation, depression, and a variety of different human experiences we can label akin to death. Perhaps it's moving. Perhaps it's the death of a loved one. All of these can become event archetypes for the experiences that we are having.

Separation from Parents

This is an important experience in our life span. You can see that this correlates with developmental psychology. It's understanding of the various life stages and developmental tasks that people have. Obviously, separation from parents is a significant experience. Some people look forward to that. Some people are forced into that proposition. Some people have difficulty with that.

Interestingly, these archetypes have even made television shows—one called *Mama's Boy*—where they show relationships wherein the man in any given relationship has been unable to separate from his parents. This is obviously a significant developmental issue.

We see as a metaphor an archetypal event that people might feel ripped from themselves or ripped from their parents, or forced into change. All these things can be elements of this archetype initiation. It's creating a community of some experience of connecting with something. It could be a vocational choice. It could be people joining all kinds of community and civic clubs and organizations to feel a sense of belonging and a part of things. Initiation is acceptance, leadership, and participation, initiation into the many different aspects of life experience.

Marriage

Marriage is an archetypal event and culturally universal. It's practiced virtually in every society in many cases in the same way with similar rituals and similar contracts, and similar beliefs. Marriage is well-defined and well-understood as an archetypal event.

The Union of Opposites

This is the anima and animus, the masculine and the female side, and they must join together. Dr. Jekyll and Mr. Hyde are the good and evil parts of us when the opposites join together. If you are interested in Chinese philosophy, there is the Tao and the idea of the yin and yang and that opposites always coexist and nothing ever occurs in isolation without a complementary or opposite side. This is really an interesting idea that is certainly not a new idea. Jung was writing about this a hundred years ago. Guiguzi, *The Sage of Ghost Valley*, was writing about this several thousand years ago.

These are the archetypal events that Jung talks about. He then discusses archetypal personas. These are people that our clients will identify with as being a part of. In Jungian psychology, we see a part of us is this archetype. The archetypes, of course, are the mother figure, the father figure, and the child figure.

Of course, John Bradshaw focused on that child within us, the devil persona, and that bad side of us. Maybe it's even the shadow self, the god persona, and that part of us that is knowing, loving, caring, or whatever other archetypes we associate with this god character—the wise old man, the wise old woman.

One of my favorite songs of all time was a Nat King Cole song, "Nature Boy." One of those lines in the song is about meeting a wise old man, the boy in the song,

"And while we spoke of many things

Fools and kings

This he said to me

The greatest thing you'll ever learn

Is just to love and be loved in return."

We can see this archetype of the wise old man giving advice or sharing wisdom and experiences. Jung recognized, long before feminism, the wise old woman and the importance of that wise old woman.

For me, it was my grandmother. My grandmother was a wise old woman. I was lucky enough to have my grandmother well into my forties before she finally passed away at age ninety-six. I hear her speaking to me still. A part of me identifies with my grandmother—the wise old woman.

Then we have another archetype—the trickster. This is the jokester, jester, merrymaker, and fun maker. This could become a defense mechanism, by the way, and also be a way of creating social engagement and experiences.

Then there is the hero that we see, of course, in every movie but that we all see within ourselves. So we have this archetype of our own personality.

The archetypal motifs or themes are the themes of deluge, overwhelm, creation, being able to do things, autonomy, and the archetype of the apocalypse, and how it will all end and how to make meaning out of madness.

These archetypes that Jung gives us are valuable for us to study because they inform parts therapy. Yes. It can give me labels: the wise old man, the devil, the god within us, the child within us, etc. But as I'm working with a client, and they're sharing their experiences with me, and I'm attending, listening, and paying attention to what it is that they're expressing, they're often expressing the crossroads that they face at an archetypal event with an archetypal persona or wrestling with an archetypal motif. They're trying to make sense of it and emerge from the other side. They're trying to leave an experience behind due to their interaction with the archetype and emerge on the other side with a problem solved.

CHAPTER TWENTY-ONE:

Perspectives on Carl Jung

I want to share a modern conceptualization of Jung's ideas and Jungian archetypes. These are the ideas of Margaret Mark and Carol Pearson. They have written numerous books and discussed the idea of Jungian archetypes at great length. Their model of Jungian archetypes is actually a very popular understanding. You'll probably see it as Jungian psychology, which it is, but it comes from Margaret Mark and Carol Pearson.

It begins with four ordinal propositions or ordinal orientations: the ego, order, freedom, and social. In other words, for the ordinal propositions, the archetypes within that are going to serve a certain purpose.

The Ego

The ego is that part of us that wants to be seen. It's the part of us that has admiration, the part of us that has a position, that knows the position, that part of us that is public, that part of us that is often the leading part of our personality. It might be how others describe our persona.

According to Mark and Pearson, within the ego is the hero archetype, the magician or the outlaw, and these archetypes are actually serving the purposes of the ego.

Order

This is our deep need for structure, for order. This allows us to function within communities and societies, within cultures, within the law, and within the context of religious ideas. All of these are things that come from our need for order. This might be the part of us that is the archetype of the caregiver, the creator, or the ruler.

Freedom

Many years ago, I was with a friend on Khreshchatyk Avenue in downtown Kyiv, Ukraine. It's a place that's very close and dear to my heart. I had spent several weeks in Ukraine. I had numerous experiences while I was there that really did change my life. The people and the friends that I met are still people and friends that are an important part of my life today.

My friend asked me, "Are Americans like Ukrainians?" I remember not answering right away. We continued to walk. We walked past break-dancers dancing on the street long after break-dancing was not cool anymore. We listened to musicians playing Frank Sinatra's "My Way" on the cello. We walked through the subway and train stations and passed McDonald's in Maidan Square and the fountains.

Finally, I answered the question. I said, "Yes. Ukrainians are exactly like Americans." My friend asked, "In what way?" "Ukrainians and Americans are just like everyone else. We all have two needs. Those are the need to experience love—to love ourselves, love other people, have a sense of love, and have a sense of freedom."

Yes. Ukrainians are just like Americans. They want freedom and love just like everyone else in the world.

Mark and Pearson recognized that freedom is one of those ordinal presuppositions that the goal of the archetype is to meet our need for freedom. This can be the explorer, the innocent, and the sage, all contributing to developing a sense of freedom from within.

Social

This could be the jester, the lover, the member, the social need to create connection, the social need for a sense of belonging, or the social need to avoid isolation and loneliness and become a part of other people around us.

Mark and Pearson identify as one of the ordinal presuppositions the idea that a part of us is striving for freedom.

This modern conceptualization of Jung's work is presented in the diagram below. We can put the archetypes your clients might identify either with this label or with a different label as being operational in their experiences. We can see that their deepest needs are being met through the emergence of this part of their personality in the work they are doing.

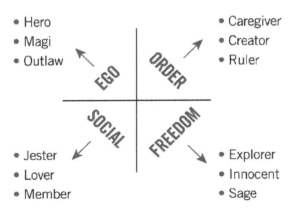

JUNGIAN ARCHETYPES
(Margaret Mark & Carol Pearson)

- Hero
- Magi
- Outlaw

EGO   *ORDER*

- Caregiver
- Creator
- Ruler

SOCIAL   *FREEDOM*

- Jester
- Lover
- Member

- Explorer
- Innocent
- Sage

CHAPTER TWENTY-TWO:

Shadow Work

The shadow self and going through a process of discovering, integrating, and assimilating the shadow part of our personality is one of the core foundations of Carl Jung's work. It really encapsulates the quote by Carl Jung, "What is not brought to consciousness, comes to us as fate." In other words, if we do not discover the shadow side of ourselves, if we don't understand this part, if we don't do the work, it actually ends up becoming our fate. It's what will do us in.

The important thing to know about shadow work is that it's not a single session activity. This is something that people go through throughout their lives. I'll share with you some methods you can use in working with your clients. I'm also going to share some personal experiences as well as some historical examples so that you craft and create, whether it's coaching, counseling, or hypnosis sessions with your clients, results that produce long-term goals.

Let's return to the idea of hypnosis and hypnotherapy, which is often marketed and sold as a quick cure or a quick solution. Recognize that hypnosis can be a fast pathway to finding results, especially when dealing with stress, anxiety, pain control, or habit control.

But as an aspect of long-term therapy with an individual, there's absolutely no shame in doing extended work with individuals, giving them an opportunity both in counseling and coaching or in hypnosis to work on the shadow shelf. This is what really brings a person from the point of adequate functioning to the point of peak performance.

I talk about the concept of different models in traditional counseling or therapy as it's practiced in the current era of managed care and third-party reimbursement. We take people who have a diagnosis; they're often in crisis. We're trying to help them rise to an adequate level of functioning. In coaching, we're often taking people at an inadequate level of functioning and helping them rise to their highest self to a level of peak performance.

That is fundamentally what the difference is between counseling and coaching. Both models use, in large part, the same set of skills.

Although shadow work can take a dysfunctional person and help them move to a functional level, in reality, I think it's far more effective to take a person who is functioning adequately and use other methods of therapy to bring a person from crisis to stabilization. Then your shadow work is a long-term approach to help people rise to their highest level of performance.

The first goal of our work is to help a person encounter their shadow. This can be done in meditation. This can be done in therapy and hypnosis. And all three of those approaches may actually use some of these same methods.

One of the ways to help a person encounter the shadow is to help them begin paying attention to themselves. This is, of course, a hallmark of contextual psychology, mindfulness-based approaches, solution-focused brief therapy, and even cognitive-behavioral therapy.

In hypnosis, I can help people discover their shadow self when their eyes are closed, and they're in a deep level of trance to see themselves as they truly are, allowing a person's subconscious mind to bring to the conscious awareness their attributes that they're not in harmony with, incongruent with, or that they have rejected from themselves.

Trancework is a beautiful time to explore and simply sit with a client, sometimes in silence, as the subconscious mind identifies the elements or the aspects of the dark shadow or the shadow self.

Notice that I just used the phrase "dark shadow." When we talk about Jungian psychotherapy, we often talk about the dark shadow. This is where shame resides. This is the part of the person that they would rather not be. This is the part of a person they feel least connected to and sometimes have difficulty recognizing that it's a part of who they are.

For the first forty-five years of my life, I always cast myself as a very empathetic person, as a person who was able to put myself in the experiences or the frame of mind of others. I could easily walk with people.

That seems to be the antithesis of how I would describe myself today. One of the ways I describe myself at age fifty-six is fairly narcissistic. I had to understand that the narcissistic self was a dark shadow. Many of the problems I created for myself in the first 80 percent of my life were actually caused by not paying attention to and recognizing this narcissistic self—this dark shadow I have carried with me over the last ten years.

I've done a lot of work in this area. I've begun to engage in the second task of merging with the shadow so my empathetic self and my narcissistic self can coexist, resulting in assimilation. What we mean by assimilation is the ability to have what I've referred to as advanced parallel programming. I wrote about this together with R. J. Banks in *Advanced Parallel Programming and the Law of Attraction*. This is where our shadow and ideal selves are in a parallel relationship. They no longer cause crashes at the intersection that has no stop signs.

Once I recognized that I was not always the benevolent Richard but was also a narcissistic Richard that affected my parenting, my romantic relationships, my business, and my personal satisfaction, it was an epiphany. Using one of Jung's archetypes was a birth for me of awareness. It helped me be a more effective therapist, a more effective father, a more effective spouse, colleague, and business partner.

How does this come about where we can encounter the shadow? I love dream work. I believe that dreams are representations of our subconscious experiences and that people want to attach meaning to their dreams. If you dream about a car, it means you are speeding through life. If you dream about a cloud, it means you are deeply relaxed. I don't think we can define for each person that a cloud means this and the ocean means that.

What we have instead is the randomness of our unconscious mind. They say we have fifty thousand thoughts a day. These thoughts are fragments of a sentence, a word, or just an ethereal feeling. When we go to sleep, what's happening is the mind's mental cachet is being cleared out. Those parts and fragments are coming to the surface.

I love asking my clients, "What did you dream of last night?" I ask my clients to keep a dream journal. It's a great exercise that can help a person bring to their awareness, identify, and encounter the shadow so they can begin to merge with the shadow.

The dark shadow, these things we'd rather not have as representations of ourselves, are things that we need to recognize as a part of ourselves. That is what merging with it means. When I recognize that part of my shadow self is narcissism, I have hope. I can have hope because I recognize that I must pay greater attention to others and the impact on their lives. It lets me know that I have limits and need to pay attention to those limits to be respectful of the other people around me.

By merging with the shadow and recognizing that the empathetic Richard is there, but so is the narcissistic Richard, I can, at age fifty-six, live in a state of parallel programming where the two aspects, the yin or the yang, or the Tao of my personality, are coexisting. It was Guiguzi who told us that it doesn't matter if the door is opened or closed. There is opportunity on both sides of the door.

When we talk about Jungian psychology, we talk about the dark self. But there is also the "golden shadow." The golden shadow is what Jung described as our suppressed creativity. It's often what we see in others that we wish we had in ourselves.

We can go back to Sigmund Freud. We can ask, "How does this develop while the golden self develops?" Maybe you were a creative kid, and you were doing all these things. But your parents told you, "Hey, you need to pay attention at school. You have to do math. You have to do your homework. You need to stop playing the piano. You need to quit writing music. You need to stop painting so you can focus. Stop writing poetry so you can focus on those things you're supposed to do."

The golden shadow is that part of us that was suppressed. Unlike shame which resides in the dark shadow, potential lives in our golden shadow.

Shadow work is not necessarily all about the dark, horrible parts of us that we don't like. But the process of shadow work is, I believe, a lifetime process. I'm looking forward to the next fifty-six years of recognizing the fragments of my shadows that I've suppressed, both my golden shadows and my dark shadows and doing that with methods like journaling and dream awareness. Sometimes I see my own experiences in the lives of others.

This is why *The Big Book* of Alcoholics Anonymous or even Alcoholics Anonymous itself is a social phenomenon. It's so powerful. People go to a meeting. They have what we call in alcohol-and-drug-abuse counseling "terminal uniqueness." They believe that nobody is like them. They encounter a whole room of people who are just like them.

As the individuals share in a meeting, a person who comes into a meeting sees themselves in the lives of others.

This is the value of storytelling in therapy. Every therapist should strive to become a master storyteller. This is a hypnotic method of therapy, by the way. Good hypnotists tell stories, metaphors, parables, Aesop's Fables, stories from their own experiences, stories from the lives of others, and stories from the popular press. All these things can help create a narrative so that an individual can see themselves and become a mirror into the lives of others. Jung was an influential figure in Alcoholics Anonymous.

I want to briefly discuss the shadow self in relation to the case of Rowland H. Alcoholics Anonymous was co-founded by "the healer" Bill Wilson (known as Bill W.) and Robert Smith (known as Dr. Bob) in 1935. But preceding that was a religious group that was called the Oxford Group. This was a meeting in Akron, Ohio, headed by an Evangelical Christian group. Alcoholics Anonymous became a non-sectarian solution to alcohol abuse that grew out of the Oxford Group.

Rowland H. was an American businessman who sought help for his addiction and alcoholism. He went to see Carl Jung in Switzerland. Jung worked with him. He said, "Hey, we've done all this psychiatry, but you're at the end of the psychiatric limits of me being able to help you. What you need is you need to have a vital spiritual experience." He told Rowland to go back to America, find a religious group, and have a spiritual awakening because there was nothing else, he said, that could help him.

Rowland went to the Oxford Group, where he had what he believed was a vital spiritual experience. He was able to stay sober. He was involved in the founding of Alcoholics Anonymous. The story of Rowland is in *The Big Book* of Alcoholics Anonymous.

In 1961, shortly before Jung's death, Bill Wilson wrote to Jung, thanking him for his early contributions. He received a response from

Jung that became a cornerstone or a foundation of looking at the shadow self as part of addiction recovery.

Addiction recovery could be concerning alcohol, any drug of abuse, a behavior, or nicotine abuse. It could be anything that a person becomes addicted to; the Home Shopping Network, day trading, etc., whatever it is where the action becomes a distraction.

In the context of alcoholism, Jung said that it was a faux, fake, or poor attempt to create a spiritual experience. A "faux spiritual experience." The person drinks in order to have a vital spiritual experience. But because it's not a real spiritual experience, it just continues the problem.

How do we create a vital spiritual experience? A vital spiritual experience could occur in a religious context. Religion can be a way of meeting our spiritual needs. But even people who are not religious experience a vital spiritual experience. I think Jung was talking about that when referring to having a vital spiritual experience: encountering the shadow, merging with the shadow, and assimilating with the shadow.

What Carl Jung is talking about here is, in the context of the spiritual experience, the power of discovering that shadow self, merging with that shadow self, and assimilating into that shadow self.

Below I present a meditation/hypnosis to help you pay attention to your shadow self and begin to encounter the shadow, merge with the shadow, and assimilate with the shadow:

"With your eyes closed down, take in a breath, pay attention to this moment in your awareness. Pay attention to the chair below you where you sit. Pay attention to my voice as you hear it. You can even scan your body anywhere, the physical part of you that is carrying the tension of the day. You can let that tension melt away.

It is in this place of paying attention to the here and now that we can begin to create a journey or an encounter with that shadow self, those parts of us where we have hidden our true self not only from others but from ourselves.

Imagine that where you are sitting right now next to you on the floor is a shadow being cast by the sun behind you. That shadow extends out in front of you. That shadow of you sitting in the chair directly in front of you is a tall, long shadow of you because the reality is the shadow personality. The shadow part is a large part of who we are, and we are carrying this with us.

In this time and this space, as you imagine paying attention to the shadow, you can ask yourself what parts are within that shadow? What part would you never share with anyone else? What part would make you feel humiliated if someone were to discover it? What part have you spent your whole life fighting against not becoming that part?

Pay attention to the shadow—it may be uncomfortable to do this—by paying attention to the different parts of the shadow, looking all the way to the top of the shadow, where the head is, all the way to the starting point of the shadow where your feet are. Then recognize that many different components or parts of the shadow are present. This is the beginning of really encountering the shadow, simply recognizing that 'it is present with me.' No matter where you go, as long as there is light, we actually have a shadow. That shadow is actually us. It is our self which is why no matter where we go, we discover we have to go with ourselves.

In this moment, in this time that you've set aside for learning, imagine. Imagine that the sun behind you moves. The sun behind you moves to a different position in the sky. The shadow becomes closer and closer and closer to you. As the shadow becomes closer and closer and as the sun sets behind you, you discover something interesting; that shadow simply becomes a part of the darkness of the night that surrounds us. Recognize that those parts that we saw outside of us and the shadow in front of us are now simply around us and in us in the darkness of night.

With the conscious mind, this might even seem like a scary thought. But with the unconscious mind, there is a sense of acceptance. Acceptance does not mean we like something. We endorse it. We are glad these bad parts are there. We recognize that there really is no such thing as bad parts. There are simply parts of us that are different than other parts. They can become a part of us, merging with ourselves in the evening hours and in the nighttime hours of life, giving some opportunity when the morning comes.

The shadow comes from the other side. As the shadow is cast from the other side, going in the opposite direction, we can see how the parts of our shadow self can be used in a new and different way, that we can—if we're talking about the golden shadow—tap into that creativity that has lain dormant for so long and use them to strengthen resources that were elements of our shadow self, our dark self, that allow us to create new boundaries, new limits, new awareness, and new connections with the people in the world around us.

Even though this has only been a short four-or-five-minute meditational process, you can sense right now the power of really being open to the idea of exploring the shadow self, the ability to merge with those parts. It is much easier than trying to get rid of those parts and assimilating those parts into a useful and resourceful set of strategies that can help us rise to our highest level of performance.

Take in a breath. As you are taking a breath, allow yourself to feel a sense of aliveness, a sense of energy. When I count to three, open your eyes. One, two, three. Opening the eyes, a smile on the face, recognizing that the shadow is us."

CHAPTER TWENTY-THREE:

Eliciting New Parts

An exciting idea goes along with all that we have discussed to this point. That is the idea of eliciting new parts.

Why would we want to elicit new parts? You've probably heard a client say, "It feels like there's a part of me missing." Well, when you hear a client tell you that, what they are saying is, "I'm looking for a part of me that I can't access or find."

There are a few reasons why this is true. First, we're dealing with a part that has gone, that is repressed, that is inward, that they can no longer find, discover, tap into, or utilize. What we really have here is a part of them that is returning. This may be an experience that the client might relate to you in grief, a part of the grieving process, maybe even a part of them that is no longer present.

We're really seeking to return that part to their experience. There are some ways that we can go about doing that.

ELICITING NEW PARTS

+ A PART THAT IS `RETURNING`
+ A PART THAT IS IN `OTHERS`
+ A PART THAT `NEVER EXISTED`

- Write letters of initiation
- The welcome parts
- Get the other parts to get it

- Identify that part
- Access resources already present to support that part
- Imagine that part coming to the table

- P.A.R.T.S
- Open space
- Action

The second reason we might want to elicit a new part is that that part is in others. In Alcoholics Anonymous, newcomers seek out a sponsor. They seek out a sponsor, being told that the sponsor has something they want: an attribute or characteristic, a part of themselves that they see in somebody else that they wish was present in their own life. We can see that we can elicit a new part by seeing these parts in other people.

The third element of this could be a part that has never existed. A client may recognize that they are limited in their ability to accomplish or do what they need to because this part does not yet exist. The question is whether the therapy can re-elicit new parts, either returning parts, parts discovered in others, or parts that never existed. The answer to that is yes. There are a number of strategies for doing this.

Let's take a look at the part that's returning. There are several different therapeutic techniques that we could utilize to invite a part of us that's no longer present to become associated again. We're looking to bring this hidden part, this distant part, this absent part, back to our experience and connect it to the associated part, the part that's in the present moment.

We can do that in several ways.

The first strategy is to have my client write a letter of invitation to that part. They can take out a pen and paper and write:

"Dear Part, it's been a long time since we've been together. I found that in the past, this was beneficial. Perhaps another part of me pushed you aside. Or perhaps, in our experience at that time, you were left behind. But I'd like to extend an invitation to you to return."

This writing process is very powerful. Words and written words, in particular, have meaning. I love giving my clients the assignment to write written affirmations. I want clients to write journals because it's them in their own handwriting, seeing in their own words what they want and need. It's a really powerful self-confrontation.

Writing this letter of invitation to that part that's no longer with us is a very powerful mechanism for having a person move to a resource state of being able to associate into it once again in the present moment. This can be given as a therapeutic homework assignment between sessions. It can be done in the middle of a session. It can be done in the middle of a hypnosis session. It can be composed with pencil and paper or with a keyboard and screen. But it can actually be done metaphorically as well as the client works through the process of how they would word it and what they would put in that invitation.

The second element of this, if we want to have a part that is returning, is to create a celebration for that part and to celebrate that part returning through the format of a welcome party. In hypnosis, you can see how this is easily done. Imagine we have done an induction and deepener.

"In this moment, recognize the value of that part that once was. Imagine in your mind's eye a welcoming party for that part that is returning home, that part that is having dust uncovered and is returning. Welcome that part with the other parts of you, recognizing how the returning part is once again welcome."

We can do this in really any number of different ways. One of my favorite strategies is asking the other part to go get it. This is a really cool mechanism in therapy. It can be produced at any point by simply saying:

"The part that is missing has been gone for a long time. Let me ask, are there some parts present who would be willing to go and get that part and bring it back? Tell me what your journey is like? What are you doing along the way? What is your progress toward getting that part back? What is it like bringing that part back with you?"

Of course, this could culminate back into the welcome party. Or these other parts could literally carry that invitation with it. These are some great strategies we can bring into our therapy for a part that is returning.

Let's take a look at a part that is in others. When you think about other people and the parts that they have that we wish were a part of us, we can identify what that part is.

For example, let's say we're working with the CEO of a worldwide hotel. This individual is a great community leader and an excellent CEO.

Let's now imagine that in the process of discovering parts that are in others, there is the leadership part of this CEO. Perhaps the CEO tells you, "I'm feeling that there is a part of me that's absent, that doesn't have those same leadership qualities," whatever they might be, anything ranging from emotional intelligence to the ability to communicate.

We identify the part that we want in another person, in this case, leadership. I want to access the resources already present to support that part. I would ask my client:

"What parts are present that can support a leader? What is present right now that could be involved in really wooing or convincing that part to join your team?"

I might have them look inside and discover that there's a part that's an effective communicator. There's a part that cares about other people. There is a part that wants to be the best. There is a part that recognizes the importance of creating a legacy.

Once I identify the resources and the other parts to support that, I can imagine that part coming from someone else and becoming a part of me. This does not mean it has to leave them, and they no longer have that part. This is a great thing about the imagination.

Another leadership part could emerge from that mentor or from that learning experience and become its own part, joining our team. This is an effective visualization, an effective creative strategy, and an effective way of associating in our present state the parts of others that could be beneficial or resourceful to us.

Let's take a look here at the last element, parts that never existed. If somebody says, "I've always felt that there's a part of me that's missing," let's look at it from the PARTS model discussed earlier.

- What are the **p**hysical aspects of that part?
- What are the **a**ssociated parts? What are they agreeing with? What is obvious? What is present?
- What are the **r**epressed parts? What are the parts of that part that are not seeing the shadow parts?
- What are the parts that are the **t**eam players and are willing essentially to join the team?
- What are the **s**ymbolic parts? What does it mean? What is the significance of this part?

I can identify in my mind a clear representation of a part using the PARTS model. Then I can simply engage in the process of opening space. This is often done through mindfulness meditation, other forms of meditation such as Trātaka, or other focused meditation. It can be done in a hypnotic state. It can simply be done cognitively and intellectually as an exercise in our own mind, resulting in an action that invites.

I love the invitation to the banquet room as a metaphor for the invitation. I would describe that to my client this way:

"Imagine now being seated at a banquet table at the head of the table. You are sitting at this table with all of your parts. You are enjoying the festivities of the experience of the harmonious sharing of resources between each one of these parts. Maybe these resources are represented by apples at this banquet or by slices of delicious and expensive food at this banquet, whatever we want to put on the banquet table.

Imagine though there is one chair open. We are still waiting for one guest to arrive. At some point in the process, that guest arrives and is then seated at the table."

In my own experiences, I found a great visualization for this: I'm at the head of the table. That's my associated self. The other parts are surrounding the table. At the far end of the table is the open chair for me to make eye-to-eye contact with that part, whether that part is a returning part, whether that is a part from others that is being shared with me, or whether that is a part that never existed but has now joined the table.

BIBLIOGRAPHY

Bradshaw, J. (1992). *Homecoming: Reclaiming and championing your inner child*. Bantam Books.

Emmerson, G. (2007). *Ego state therapy*. Crown House.

Herbine-Blank, T., & Sweezy, M. (2021). *Internal Family Systems couple therapy skills manual: Healing relationships with intimacy from the inside out*. PESI Publications.

Jung, C. G. (1981). *The archetypes and the collective unconscious*. Princeton University Press.

Jung, C. G., & Hinkle, B. M. (2003). *Psychology of the unconscious*. Dover Publications.

Martel, R. (2020). *The magic of aesop: How to use the wisdom of Aesop's Fables to spark transformational change*. MagicofAesop.com.

Schwartz, R. C. (2021). *No bad parts: Healing trauma and restoring wholeness with the internal family systems model*. Sounds True.

van der Kolk, B. (2015). *The body keeps the score: Brain, mind, and body in the healing of trauma*. Penguin Books.

Zarren, J. I., & Eimer, B. N. (2002). *Brief cognitive hypnosis: Facilitating the change of dysfunctional behavior*. Springer.

Made in the USA
Monee, IL
30 January 2023

26773942R00094